The Art of Dining in Memphis 2

Italian Billini Salad Set from Brookhaven Antiques Shop

a Restaurant Guide with Signature Recipes

Bon Appétit!
Joy Bateman

Joy Bateman

author illustrator publisher

www.joysartofdining.com

3

To my loving husband, Bill, who has shown the patience of Job while I worked for hours on end to complete this book while also working at *Memphis* magazine; and to my caring parents for their phenomenal ability to draw out the creativity in all our family members.

Thanks to Pamela and Margaret for their hard work: Pamela McFarland, a gentle soul and my creative, expert graphic artist; and Margaret Pellett, my copy editor and research assistant, whose efforts never cease to amaze me.

My appreciation goes to The Booksellers at Laurelwood (formerly Davis-Kidd Booksellers) who almost ceased to be. Thank you for keeping all my books in the limelight, right out front!

The Art of Dining in Memphis 2
Library of Congress Cataloging-in-Publishing Data
ISBN 978-0-9773226-3-3

$21.95 plus S & H

Printed in the United States of America

For those that love it, cooking is at once child's play and adult joy. CRAIG CLAIBORNE

Dear Reader,

I like the way Chinese speakers greet one another, according to Rick Stein in *Words from the Wise*: "Not strictly saying, 'hello,' but 'have you eaten yet?'" They're speaking my language. The next question would be, where can one find mouthwatering, feverishly flavorful fare?

Memphis is the answer. In recent years, Memphis restaurateurs are successfully appealing to more discerning palates. As a lifelong Memphian, I am especially excited about this second book about dining in Memphis. I will guide you through some excellent restaurants and offer you signature recipes to try at home.

So many restaurants, so little time and space… Unable to include all my favorite Memphis restaurants in this short guide, I want to mention a few top dining destinations that are not featured, even a few places that are now history.

No need to mention BBQ , really, but I will share my favorites: The Bar-B-Q Shop, Central BBQ , Corky's and the Rendezvous. Fantastic. Back in the 60's there was Shorty's BBQ on Summer Avenue. Nothing could beat it. I rode my J.C. Higgins English bicycle almost every weekend to get their incredible BBQ sandwich. Occasionally, I would have a small carton of buttermilk, too. I could see this was the drink of choice among the construction workers and other men who were there for the BBQ. Shorty's was very small, with just enough old wooden school-desks to seat 6 or 7 diners.

Stepping up to the present day, I know that fried chicken is the latest in retro chic: Two very young chefs are perfecting it. My grandsons, Ben and Alex, have been making spicy chicken legs since they were just out of the crib, and they are passionate about their work.

Moving straight from the simple to the sublime, I'd like to direct your attention to the Split Pea Soup and Crispy Lemon Chicken Paillard with Petite Salad Parmesan served at River Oaks, the restaurant owned by Master Chef José Gutierrez. In March, 2011, Chef Gutierrez received the Toque d'Argent-Trophée André Surmain, which is the Chef of the Year award from the Maîtres Cuisiniers de France. Take note: River Oaks.

Japan is a long way from Memphis, but near the corner of Cooper and Young, Karen Carrier's restaurant Dō Sushi + Noodles serves up sushi that's hard to beat.

The Little Tea Shop on Monroe has some of the best, healthiest southern home-style cooking around. A generous portion of chicken salad with avocado on a bed of fresh lettuce is heart-stoppingly delicious. Soups, seriously hearty! A great place for a quick business lunch where one might see some of the who's-who of Memphis.

Chef David Johnson, formerly of McEwen's on Monroe and (the sorely missed) Jarrett's, has recently opened a small spot called Southern Belle, with a limited menu of delectable items to eat-in or take-out. On Mondays, the Red Beans and Rice with Cajun Smoked Sausage is Crescent City soul food.

Memphis restaurateurs know that diners want very fresh, locally sourced ingredients whenever possible. Attention all grocery shoppers: The Memphis Farmer's Market (Downtown) and our very own local grocer, Easy-Way®, family owned and operated since 1932, are excellent sources of high quality local products.

My sweet tooth insists that I mention Dinstuhl's. Purveyors of fine candies in Memphis since 1902, the Dinstuhl family helps Memphians celebrate the arrival of spring each year with their famous Chocolate Covered Strawberries.

The Art of Dining in Memphis 2 should help you become better informed about where to eat and what to eat. You will be able to answer the Chinese greeting, "Have you eaten yet?" in the affirmative, or you will know where next to dine.

Look out New Orleans! Look out Chicago! Memphis is becoming a top regional dining destination!

Enjoy!

Joy Bateman

www.joysartofdining.com

Table of Contents

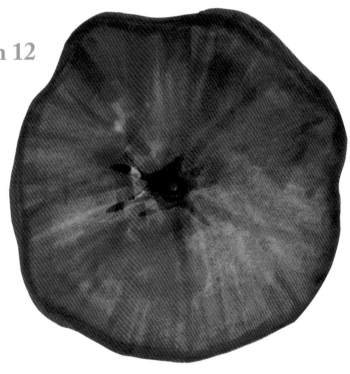

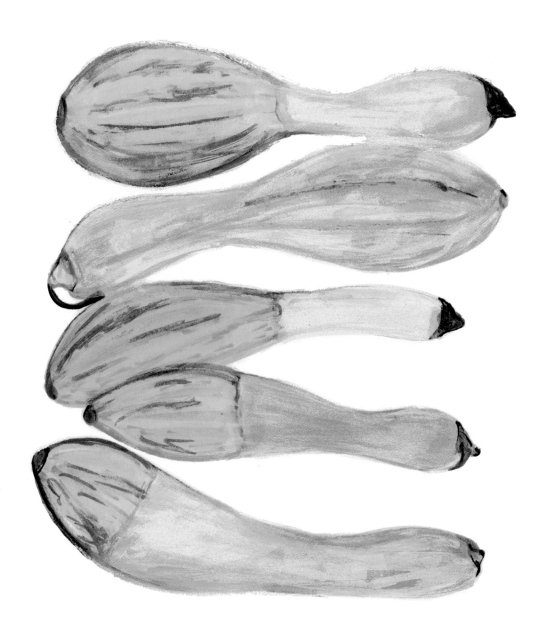

Local foodies watched and waited impatiently as the original house underwent extensive renovation and the acre of land was transformed into a lush garden. Before Acre even opened, area foodies were excited. Chefs Wally Joe and Andrew Adams are well known in the region. The cuisine is Classical French with hints of Italy, Asia and the American South. "I insist on using the absolute best ingredients available and do as little as possible to them," says Chef Wally Joe. Acre opened to rave reviews and the word is out: Exceptional! My awesome first course was Peekytoe Crab Cake with "Salad of Carrots, Daikon Sprouts, Sesame Whole Grain Mustard Vinaigrette, Shisso & Apple," served with warm French bread. My entrée, Seared Sea Scallops with "Zucchini, Squash, Roasted Tomatoes and ACRE Garden Butter," was remarkable. For me, sea scallops are a must-order at Acre. Dessert was a delicious and memorable part of the meal: Sticky Toffee Date Cake with Vanilla Gelato, a perfect grand finale. Private dining available; outdoor dining, first-come-first-served, in season.

Gnocchi Verdi with Cherry Tomatoes, Sage and Red Wine Brown Butter Sauce

Yield: 6 servings

Part I: Ricotta Gnocchi

Ingredients:
1 cup ricotta cheese
1 egg
½ cup semolina flour, plus extra for rolling
¼ cup blanched, finely chopped spinach

Method:
Mix all ingredients and knead slightly. If too wet, add more semolina flour.

On a semolina dusted table, gently roll dough into several snake shaped ropes about ½" in diameter.

Cut the ropes of dough into pieces 1" in length.

Bring a large pot of salted water to a boil.

Drop gnocchi into the boiling water one at a time and cook in small batches.

When gnocchi are done, they rise to the top of the water. As the gnocchi surface, remove them with a slotted spoon and transfer them to a large serving bowl. Be on the alert for gnocchi

that may be stuck to the bottom of the pot, and gently pry them loose with the slotted spoon.

Repeat for all batches.

Part II: Red Wine Brown Butter

Ingredients:
3 Tbs red wine vinegar
1 cup red wine
1 minced shallot
1 sprig fresh tarragon
½ cup vegetable broth
1 stick (¼ lb) butter

Method:

In a saucepan, bring vinegar, red wine, minced shallot, and tarragon to a simmer; reduce to about 1 Tbs liquid: The pan will be almost dry. Remove from heat and set aside.

In a separate pan, heat butter over medium heat until it just starts to brown and give off a nutty aroma. Remove from heat and set aside.

Separately, heat vegetable broth to a simmer and transfer to a blender container.

With the blender running, very slowly add the melted butter to the container with the vegetable broth.

Add the butter/broth mixture to the saucepan containing the wine reduction.

Mix well. Strain and reserve liquid. (Discard solids.)

Part III: Finishing the Dish

Garnishes:

1 Tbs chopped sage

1 cup halved, assorted grape tomatoes

Method:

Add Red Wine Brown Butter Sauce to bowl with Ricotta Gnocchi. Toss with 1 Tbs chopped sage and 1 cup halved grape tomatoes. Season with salt and pepper and serve.

Sugar Snap Pea Tonic

Yield: 1 serving

Ingredients:

1½ oz Hendrick's gin
1 Tbs puréed sugar snap peas (prepared in blender)
Dash of simple syrup
Dash of lime
Tonic water
1 sugar snap pea for garnish

Method:

Shake gin, pea purée, simple syrup and dash of lime together with ice.

Pour gin and ice mixture into a rocks glass.

Top with tonic water. Garnish rim of glass with a sugar snap pea.

Entering Amerigo™ I was immediately charmed by the décor: polished brass hardware, dark wood paneling, ceiling fans throughout, white tablecloths and black and white checkerboard flooring. We're here in the city of Elvis, my own hometown, but hey! Amerigo™ has that New Orleans feel and I love it. The Italian cuisine at Amerigo™ is flavorful and satisfying. The veal piccata "with white wine lemon butter sauce, gourmet mushrooms and capers over angel hair pasta with jumbo lump crabmeat"… amazing! My son, William, enjoyed the chicken Marsala. We both chowed down on Tuscan Crab Cakes with white bean salsa. baby greens and lemon basil butter sauce. As a grandmother of three toddlers, I was glad to find popular "Kids' Items" bound to entice picky little eaters. When it comes to desserts, Amerigo™ is there for us. The serving of Key Lime Pie is big enough to share with a friend. Italian treats: gelato or sorbet; tiramisu; cheesecake with fresh berries. And we're getting that New Orleans feeling again: Chocolate Bread Pudding with whisky sauce. Desserts? One of each, please.

Amerigo

1239 Ridgeway Park Place Mall Memphis, TN 761-4000 www.amerigo.net

Cheese Fritters

Yield: 12-14 servings (36 fritters @ about 3 oz each)

Ingredients:
1 cup grated Parmesan cheese
9 eggs
⅓ cup coarsely chopped fresh parsley
⅓ cup diced scallions
⅓ cup prepared horseradish
¾ cup sour cream
¼ cup minced garlic
⅛ tsp salt
⅛ tsp garlic salt
¼ tsp ground black pepper
½ tsp crushed red pepper
3 cups flour
1 ¾ lbs medium sharp cheddar cheese
1 lb cubed mozzarella cheese
1 lb cubed Swiss cheese
Vegetable oil for frying

Preparation:

In a large bowl, mix all ingredients on medium until thoroughly combined. Mixture will still be lumpy and will have the consistency of dough.

Form 36 loosely packed 3-oz cheese balls.

(Tip: A scant ⅓ cup of mixture should weigh about 3 oz.)

Add enough vegetable oil to a large, deep saucepan (or deep fryer) to reach about 2 inches in depth.

Prepare tray(s) lined with paper towels for draining cooked cheese balls. Set tray(s) where finished batches of cheese balls will stay warm while you cook remaining batches.

Heat oil to 350 degrees.

Cook cheese balls:

(Tip: Maintain proper oil temperature by cooking the cheese balls in very small batches. Avoid crowding the pan!)

1) Place several cheese balls in hot oil and fry for about 1½ minutes.

2) Flip cheese balls over and cook about 1½ minutes more, until JUST golden brown.

2) Using a slotted spoon, immediately remove finished cheese balls from oil and set to drain on paper towels.

3) Repeat for remaining batches.

Serve immediately, while hot.

Chefs Michael Hudman and Andrew Ticer attribute their passion for Italian cuisine to the influence of their Italian-American grandmothers and their large families in which every celebration "revolved around food." In 1994, Michael and Andrew began to talk about opening a restaurant. They sought out training: Johnson & Wales University; internships with French Master Chef José Gutierrez of Chez Philippe at the Peabody Hotel; the Italian Culinary Institute in Calabria, Italy. In 2008, armed with a wealth of experience and with their collection of Italian family recipes, Andrew and Michael opened their own "Italian Kitchen." All diners are seated and then welcomed with an exquisite olive mix and warm French bread. The menu changes often, but two menu standards are Truffled Chicken Livers and Maw Maw's Ravioli with meat gravy. Located in a renovated house on quiet Brookhaven Circle, Andrew Michael's offers a warm, cozy and romantic ambience for dining. Some outdoor seating; garden area in the back. Space available for special events; catering.

Andrew Michael Italian Kitchen

712 W. Brookhaven Circle Memphis, TN 347-3569 www.andrewmichaelitaliankitchen.com

Sformato with Benton* Ham Hocks, Spring Peas and Broth

Yield: 12-15 servings

Ingredients:

2 Benton* smoked ham hocks (¾ lb to 1 lb each)
6 qts cold water
Mirepoix:
    8 oz chopped onions (about 1¼ cup, ½" dice)
    4 oz diced carrots (about ¾ cup, ½" dice)
    4 oz diced celery (about 1 heaping cup, ½" dice)
1 cup butter
2 cups flour
1½ cups cream
1½ cups milk
6 eggs, separated
10 oz grated Parmesan (about 2½ cups)
1 pkg (10 oz) frozen spring peas

Method:

Preheat oven to 350 degrees.

Prepare stock:

Place ham hocks in a stock pot with 6 qts cold water. Bring to a gentle simmer, but do not allow to boil.

Add the mirepoix and continue to simmer gently for 1 hour, skimming off and discarding any scum that forms on surface.

Remove ham hocks from stock, pick off meat and discard bones.

Using 2 forks, pull chunks of meat apart into shreds, then rough chop meat and set aside.

Strain stock, discard solids and reserve broth.

Make a blond roux:

In a medium saucepan over low to medium heat, melt 1 cup butter.

Remove pan from heat momentarily, and whisk in 2 cups flour to make a smooth mixture.

Return the saucepan to the heat. Whisking and adjusting heat to keep roux from burning, cook over low to medium heat for about 5 minutes.

Whisking steadily, gradually add cream and milk to roux to make a Béchamel sauce.

Whisk the egg yolks into the Béchamel, and then incorporate the Parmesan and the rough chopped ham. Remove mixture from heat.

Whip the egg whites until medium peaks form.

Fold the whipped egg whites into the Béchamel/Parmesan/ham mixture and transfer the Sformato to an ovenproof casserole.

Bake Sformato in preheated 350 degree oven for 45 minutes. Remove casserole from oven and let rest.

Heat frozen peas in a little of the prepared broth just to warm them up. Do not overcook.

To plate:

Spoon a small portion of peas into an individual serving bowl. Place a portion of the Sformato on top.

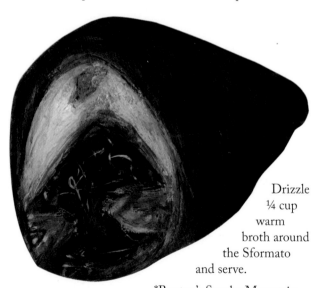

Drizzle ¼ cup warm broth around the Sformato and serve.

*Benton's Smoky Mountain Country Hams accepts telephone orders for smoked ham hocks: Tel (423) 442-5003. (Benton's accepts online orders for ham and bacon through the website, http://bentonscountryhams2.com).

One thing Memphians agree on is where to go for scrumptious Thai food. Astute restaurateur Molly Smith, Chef Sorrasit "Alex" Sittranont and the staff have served high quality, authentic Thai cuisine to thousands of diners year after year since opening the restaurant in 2002. From 2003-2011, readers of Memphis magazine awarded "Best Thai" to this extremely popular Midtown dining spot. One of my favorites, Panang Curry, with your choice of chicken, beef, pork or tofu, is served with bell pepper, sweet peas, basil and kaffir lime leaves. I prefer the chicken option. Among the House Specialties are Drunken Seafood Combination (with shrimp, squid, salmon and mussels), Crispy Duck and Salmon Panang. The beauty of the food presentation at Bhan Thai brings to my mind the term "edible art." The table settings are strikingly elegant with black napkins and black tablecloths. The orange and deep gold colored dining room walls are adorned with mirrors, decorative Thai plaques and porcelain plates. Quite large and very charming outdoor dining area. Weekends: Live entertainment on the patio, weather permitting. Banquet facilities available.

Bhan Thai ~ 1324 Peabody Memphis, TN 272-1538 www.bhanthairestaurant.com

Savory Chopped Chicken Salad

Yield: 2 servings

Ingredients:
1 ½ cups finely diced uncooked chicken
2 Tbs chopped spring onions
1 Tbs chopped coriander leaves
2 Tbs chopped mint leaves
2 Tbs sliced shallots
½ tsp dried chili flakes
1 Tbs ground roasted rice*
½ tsp salt
2 Tbs fish sauce**
2 Tbs fresh lime juice

Garnish: mint sprigs, dried chili flakes, chopped spring onion, grated Chinese cabbage and sliced shallots

Using no oil and only a pinch of salt, dry fry the diced chicken in a pan.

When the diced meat is cooked through, transfer it to a mixing bowl.

Season with chili flakes, fish sauce and lime juice. Mix well, then add ground roasted rice and stir.

Add spring onions, shallots, mint leaves and coriander. Toss to incorporate.

To serve:

Spoon chicken salad onto a serving dish. Garnish with mint sprigs, dried chili flakes, chopped spring onions, grated Chinese cabbage and sliced shallots. Serve with long beans***, spring onions and cabbage.

*Ground roasted rice (also called ground "toasted" rice) consists of Thai sticky rice that has been toasted and ground to a powder. Prepared ground roasted rice is available where Thai groceries are sold.

**Fish sauce is a condiment frequently used in Thai cooking. Bottled Thai fish sauce is sold in most Asian markets.

*** "Long beans" are green beans that grow to about 1 foot long in Southeast Asia. Shop for "long beans" in Asian markets, or substitute one of the common North American varieties of green beans.

Boscos has long been a popular destination for Sunday brunch. The mouthwatering brunch menu offers several kinds of eggs Benedict, tantalizing omelettes, Belgian waffles and desserts galore. Renowned jazz vocalist Joyce Cobb regularly performs during Sunday brunch. Starts early (10:30 a.m.); especially good for kids and grandkids. But Boscos is not just for brunch! Lunch and dinner menus feature wood-fired brick oven pizzas, fresh seafood, steaks and pastas. I ordered one of the signature appetizers, Fried Artichoke Hearts served with Buttermilk Garlic Dipping Sauce… unfreakinbelievable, arguably the single best appetizer I've had in a while. Attention beer aficionados: Boscos always keeps on tap eight of their own award winning handcrafted beers. Full bar and wine list, too.

Boscos Squared

2120 Madison Memphis, TN 432-2222 www.boscosbeer.com

Seared Ahi Tuna Salad

Yield: 4 servings

Ingredients:
4 pieces ahi (yellowfin) tuna, 5 oz each
California spring mix greens (also known as "mesclun")
½ red bell pepper, julienne cut
3 oz pickled ginger, finely chopped
½ oz wasabi
Blackened Spice (recipe below)
Sesame Ginger Dressing (recipe below)

Method:
Over each piece of tuna, pat Blackened Spice mixture to form a crust on all sides.

Preheat a large nonstick skillet over medium high heat for 2 minutes.

Place seasoned tuna pieces in skillet and sear on both sides, about 4 minutes total.

Remove tuna from pan and cool completely. (Tuna should be nicely seared on the outside and rare on the inside.)

Place greens in a large bowl. Drizzle with Sesame Ginger Dressing and toss to coat; fold in chopped ginger and julienned red bell pepper.

Arrange salad on individual plates or on a serving platter.

Cut tuna pieces into slices and fan out on top of salad. Place wasabi on side.

Blackened Spice

Ingredients:
2 Tbs Spanish paprika
1 Tbs cayenne pepper
½ Tbs white pepper
1 Tbs black pepper
1 Tbs kosher salt
½ Tbs onion powder
½ Tbs garlic powder
½ Tbs thyme

Method:
Combine all spices and mix thoroughly.

Sesame Ginger Dressing

Ingredients:
1 Tbs Dijon mustard
1 Tbs shallots
3 Tbs pickled ginger
2 Tbs fresh cilantro
2 Tbs rice wine vinegar
1 Tbs fresh lime juice
Pinch of salt
Pinch of black pepper
¾ cup olive oil
2 Tbs sesame oil

Method:
In a food processor or blender, combine the first 8 ingredients and purée until smooth. With machine still running, slowly drizzle olive oil and sesame oil into mixture to combine.

"Best Breakfast in Memphis," "Best Breakfast in the Nation" — The list of awards goes on. Rachel Ray visited Brother Juniper's and featured one of the omelets, The San Diegan, on her show "Rachel Ray's Tasty Travels" and in her book, Rachel Ray: Best Eats in Town on $40 a Day. The question is, how did Rachel Ray manage to choose just ONE. Studying the menu, I counted 26 delectable possibilities. The Spanakopita Omelet shouted out, "I'm great, choose me!" But the Desperado, an open face omelet, sweet-talked me with words of avocado spread, sautéed tomatoes, black beans, salsa, sour cream... My dream omelet. For diners with a hearty appetite indeed, I might recommend Hungry Tiger, another open face omelet, which is served on "A Bed of Home Fries Topped w/Bacon, Ham, Sausage, Tomatoes, Green Onion" and three kinds of cheese. Brother Juniper's continued success can be attributed to the innovative menu, of course, but also to the owners' strong family ties and to the community spirit the family business displays through charitable endeavors. Footnote: Brother Juniper's own spreadable fruit, coffee and sauces are for sale in the store, along with Memphis Gift Baskets stocked with local items.

Brother Juniper's

3519 Walker Memphis, TN 324-0144 www.brotherjunipers.com

Chorizo Burrito

Yield: 1 serving

Ingredients:1 flour tortilla
Small amount of chorizo sausage
Green onions, chopped
Tomatoes, chopped
3 eggs
Cooking oil
Cheddar cheese, grated
Mozzarella cheese, grated
Toppings: Salsa, sour cream, grated cheddar and chopped green onions

Warm flour tortilla on grill at low temperature.

Sauté chorizo sausage, green onions and tomatoes together; set aside.

In a separate pan over medium heat, scramble 3 eggs in light oil.

Add sautéed ingredients and grated cheeses to the scrambled eggs and mix together.

To serve:

Transfer warm tortilla to plate. Spoon egg and chorizo filling onto tortilla. Wrap tortilla around filling to form burrito. Top burrito with salsa, sour cream, grated cheddar and chopped green onions.

Note: Let personal preference determine amounts of other filling ingredients you use with the scrambled eggs. For the toppings also, let your taste be your guide.

19

The Brushmark Restaurant is located at the elegant Memphis Brooks Museum of Art. The dining room and terrace offer panoramic views of beautiful Overton Park; terrace dining is available in summer and fall. Memphians can consider themselves lucky twice — The Brushmark's Executive Chef Wally Joe and Chef de Cuisine Andrew Adams work as partners at Acre Restaurant as well. Now that I have your attention, let's talk Reubens. There are Reubens and there are Reubens. The Brushmark's Pastrami Reuben, with "House Cured Brisket … & Raisin Mustard on Rye," is simply outstanding in the field. The Brushmark Peanut Soup has for years topped the list of customer favorites. I finally tried it. No wonder people rave about this soup, rich with umami flavor. (For the soup recipe, see my first book, The Art of Dining in Memphis.) As a longtime Brushmark patron, I highly recommend the Crêpe of the Day, always delicious. The Brushmark is open for lunch Wednesday through Sunday. Open for dinner Thursdays only.

Brushmark
1934 Poplar Memphis, TN 544-6225 www.brooksmuseum.org

Shrimp Rolls

Yield: 8 sandwiches

Ingredients:
2 lbs shrimp, peeled and deveined
½ cup lemon juice, plus spent lemon halves
10 sprigs parsley, plus 2 tsp minced leaves
6 sprigs tarragon, plus 2 tsp minced leaves
2 tsp black pepper
2 small shallots, minced with SHARP knife
2 small stalks celery, minced
½ cup mayonnaise
Additional lemon juice to taste
4 avocados, pitted, peeled and chopped
Napa cabbage, shredded
8 hoagie loaves

Instructions:

In a saucepan, combine shrimp, ½ cup lemon juice, reserved lemon halves, parsley sprigs, tarragon sprigs, pepper, sugar and salt with 4 cups cold water.

Place saucepan over medium heat and cook shrimp, covered, for 8-10 minutes at EXACTLY 165 degrees.

Remove cover from saucepan; let sit for 2 minutes.

Remove shrimp from hot water and shock in ice water.

Remove shrimp from ice water and pat dry.

In a bowl, combine 2 tsp minced parsley, 2 tsp minced tarragon, minced shallots, minced celery and ½ cup mayonnaise.

Add cooked shrimp to bowl and toss to combine. Adjust seasoning to taste with additional lemon juice and salt.

Serve shrimp salad with shredded Napa cabbage and chopped avocados on toasted hoagie buns.

Blue Moon® White Bean Chili

Yield: 8-10 servings

Ingredients:
5 cloves garlic, minced
1 yellow onion, diced
3 small carrots, diced
2 stalks celery, diced
2 oz pancetta, diced
2 lbs ground turkey
1 cup milk (2% or skim)
1 22-oz Blue Moon® Belgian White Ale*
1 qt chicken stock
4 14-oz cans white beans
4 fresh sage leaves
1 Tbs white roux
2 tsp cumin
2 Tbs chili powder
1 Tbs smoked paprika

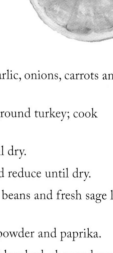

Garnishes:
1 bunch blanched, chopped mustard greens
1 cup halved grape tomatoes
Grated Monterey Jack cheese
Crumbled cornbread

Method:

In a Dutch oven, sweat garlic, onions, carrots and celery until soft.

Add diced pancetta and ground turkey; cook until browned.

Add milk and reduce until dry.

Add Blue Moon® Ale and reduce until dry.

Add chicken stock, white beans and fresh sage leaves. Cook for 1 hour.

Stir in roux, cumin, chili powder and paprika.

Garnish with one bunch blanched, chopped mustard greens, 1 cup halved grape tomatoes and grated Monterey Jack cheese.

Crumble cornbread on top to finish.

*We named this dish after a key ingredient, the Blue Moon® Belgian White Belgian-Style Wheat Ale that makes this chili special.

When proprietors Martha and Glenn Hays opened Café 1912 in 2002, they were continuing the work they started at La Tourelle, their very successful first restaurant: offering French inspired food in Midtown. Glenn takes his homework seriously, dining his way through France rather often. (It's a lotta hard work, but somebody's gotta do it.) Café 1912 warms the hearts of Francophiles in search of a bistro: the vintage deep yellow and red color scheme, classic French advertising posters, photographs of late 19th and early 20th century France, candles on every table. And the food! I had veal served over a screamingly delicious mushroom orzo pasta with a white wine, lemon and butter sauce. My Caesar salad with olive tapenade was exceptionally tasty. I am happy to report that the hearty and classic Lyonnaise salad that appeared on the café's very first menu remains on today's menu — almost a meal in itself. Serious attention is given to wine selection; the choices are very well priced. The 2008 Sonoma Cutrer Chardonnay "Russian River Ranches" is a good example. Café opens at 5:00 p.m. daily. Brunch Sundays, 11:30 a.m.—2:00 p.m. Limited outdoor seating in good weather. Bon Appétit!

Goat Cheese Ravioli

Yield: 2 ravioli

Ingredients:
1 cup Tomato Filets®*
¼ cup heavy cream
5 basil leaves
4 wonton wrappers
2 oz goat cheese
1 egg
2 cups water
Flour
2 Tbs grated
Parmesan cheese
Salt and white pepper to taste

Sauce:

In a medium saucepan, combine Tomato Filets®, cream and basil leaves.

Simmer for about 15 minutes, stirring occasionally. Remove from heat.

Pour mixture into blender and mix for about 2 minutes. Season with salt and white pepper to taste. Set aside and keep warm.

Ravioli:

Place 2 wonton wrappers on a cutting board. These will serve as base wrappers for the ravioli. Reserve the second set of wrappers to use as tops.

Roll goat cheese into two 1-oz balls. Center a cheese ball on each of the base wrappers.

In a small bowl, whisk egg and ¼ cup water together to make egg wash.

Using a pastry brush, apply egg wash to the edges of each base wrapper, where the top and bottom wrappers will be sealed together.

Onto each prepared base wrapper, place one reserved wrapper. Using your fingers, press the edges of the top and bottom wrappers together to seal the 2 completed ravioli.

Sprinkle flour over both ravioli. Let dry about 5 minutes.

In a medium saucepan, bring remaining water to a boil.

Transfer the ravioli to the boiling water and cook for about 2 minutes.

Using a slotted spoon, transfer the cooked ravioli from the water to a serving bowl.

To serve:

Pour the prepared sauce over the ravioli. Top with grated Parmesan. Enjoy.

*Tomato Filets® are canned strips of peeled tomato in juice from Stanislaus Food Products. They are sold variously as Saporito® Filetto di Pomodoro™, 74/40® Tomato Filets® and 80/40® "Robusto" Style Tomato Strips.

Pan Roasted Grouper with Beurre Blanc

Yield: 2 servings

Ingredients:
½ cup sundried tomatoes
2 Tbs sliced shallots
1 cup white cooking wine
1 cup heavy cream

2-3 Tbs butter
2 grouper fillets (6 oz each)
Salt and white pepper to taste
2 Tbs olive oil

To prepare Beurre Blanc:

Combine sundried tomatoes, shallots and white wine in a medium saucepan.

Bring to a boil and then reduce heat and simmer mixture until liquid is reduced by half (allow about 2 minutes).

Whisk in cream and heat the mixture to a boil. Reduce heat and simmer until mixture thickens slightly.

Remove pan from heat. Gradually whisk in butter. Salt to taste.

To prepare Pan Roasted Grouper:

Preheat oven to 350 degrees.

Season fillets with salt and white pepper.

Pour olive oil into a medium sized oven safe sauté pan and heat over high flame.

Place fillets in heated pan and cook for 2 minutes on each side.

Still using the sauté pan, transfer fillets to preheated 350 degree oven and cook for 6-8 minutes. Remove from oven.

To plate:

Place each fillet on a plate, top with warm Beurre Blanc and serve.

Chef's Note: Risotto is a good accompaniment for Pan Roasted Grouper.

This coffee shop, restaurant and bakery is a gathering spot for folks living in the Evergreen area, for students and staff from nearby Rhodes College and for many others as well. If only every neighborhood had this kind of cozy little hangout. Café Eclectic owner Cathy Boulden, Chef Mary O'Brien and the friendly staff pull it all together. For breakfast, I'm thrilled to get away from the conventional eggs, bacon and toast with Rachel's Breakfast Wrap, a "happy meal," for sure: "scrambled eggs, roasted peppers, caramelized onions, avocado, tomato, bacon and white cheddar." Eclectic's Eggs Florentine dish is quite special, with fresh sautéed spinach and Béchamel sauce. Lunch and dinner offerings are equally creative. Among the wraps — the Herbivore, the Italian Chicken and the Brie & Fresh Pear. Luscious salads, all with dressings prepared fresh in house. Check the bakery case right inside the café entrance for YUMMY donuts, cookies, pies, brownies, lemon bars and colorful cupcakes from the in-house bakery. Illy coffee is served. Vegetarian friendly. Takeout available, including freshly prepared picnic boxes. (On your way to the Overton Park Zoo, perhaps?) Open daily

Café Eclectic

603 N. McLean Blvd. Memphis, TN 725-1718 www.cafeeclectic.net

Strawberry Fields Salad

Yield: 8-10 servings

Ingredients:
10 oz (1 bag) fresh spinach leaves
4 oz roasted pecans
4 oz crumbled goat cheese
12 strawberries, cleaned and quartered
Strawberry Vinaigrette (recipe below)

Method:

Wash spinach leaves, remove stems and spin leaves to dry.

Either arrange spinach, pecans, cheese and strawberries on individual salad plates or toss together in a large serving bowl.

Dress with Strawberry Vinagrette and serve immediately.

Strawberry Vinaigrette:

Ingredients:
1 cup fresh strawberries
1 Tbs granulated sugar
1 tsp salt
¼ tsp ground
white pepper
¼ cup champagne vinegar
¾ cup olive oil

Method:

Wash strawberries and remove stems and leaves.

Place strawberries in a blender container and blend to purée.

Add sugar, salt, pepper and vinegar; blend until sugar and salt dissolve.

With blender running, drizzle in oil and blend until smooth.

Chill before serving.

Snickerdoodles

Yield: 2½ dozen

Ingredients:
2¼ cups flour
2 tsp cream of tartar
1 tsp baking soda
½ tsp salt
6 oz butter, softened
2 oz shortening
1½ cups plus 3 Tbs sugar
2 eggs
1 Tbs cinnamon

Method:

Preheat oven to 400 degrees.

Whisk flour, cream of tartar, baking soda and salt together; set aside.

Using a mixer at medium speed, cream together butter, shortening and 1½ cups sugar for 1 minute.

Add eggs to butter mixture; mix at medium speed until combined (about 30 seconds).

Add flour mixture to batter; beat at low speed until just combined.

In a small bowl, combine remaining 3 Tbs sugar and 1 Tbs cinnamon; set aside.

Portion the dough out into tablespoon-sized pieces; roll into balls.

Prepare parchment-lined or oiled baking sheets.

Roll the snickerdoodle balls in the cinnamon/sugar mixture and place on the prepared baking sheets.

Bake in preheated 400 degree oven for 4-5 minutes. Rotate

baking sheets for even baking. Bake 5-6 minutes longer, until just snickerdoodles are just set.

Remove snickerdoodles from baking sheets and cool on wire racks.

For a quiet, relaxing lunch, try Café Palladio. Housed in one of Memphis' upscale antiques galleries, this little café offers handsome décor: lovely paintings, china lamps, chandeliers and even some fabulous architectural pieces salvaged from the old Anderton's East restaurant building before demolition. The café sandwich list is tempting: Southern Fried Green Tomato, Aunt Ida's Pimento Cheese, River-City Cheesesteak Panini, Chunky Chicken Salad. The salad choices are likewise appealing: Cobb Salad, Hawaiian Salad, Pear & Walnut Salad, plus quite a few more. Daily soup selections. Among the beverages, Peach Tea ranks high as a customer favorite. Delicious and refreshing, a strong contender for Best in the South. For dessert, I'm hooked on the Coconut Cake, a square of very moist yellow cake topped with white icing and tender, juicy grated coconut. Dessert first, anyone? Open for lunch Tuesday – Saturday.

Café Palladio

2169 Central Ave. Memphis, TN 278-0129 www.thepalladiogroup.com

Chicken Salad for Sandwiches

Yield: Filling for about 10 sandwiches

Ingredients:
1 lb boneless, skinless chicken breasts
¾ cup pineapple juice
¼ cup Worcestershire sauce
½ cup honey
½ cup pecan pieces, chopped according to preference
¾ cup sliced seedless red grapes
Salt and pepper to taste
Enough mayonnaise to bind salad ingredients

Instructions:

Refrigerate chicken breasts overnight in a marinade of pineapple juice, Worcestershire and honey.

The next day, smoke chicken breasts in a smoker (or boil chicken, if you prefer).

Chop prepared chicken into small pieces.

Stir together chopped chicken, chopped pecans and sliced grapes.

Season with salt and pepper to taste.

Incorporate just enough mayonnaise to bind.

Bon appétit!

Some things never change. The Café Classic Seafood Bisque that has been on the menu for over twenty years is a prime example. But my heavens, this soup "is to die for!" So is the Bacon Wrapped Shrimp, baked with a creamy horseradish sauce. Fish at Café Society is always delectable---very fresh and swimming in butter. As the Polish proverb says, "Fish, to taste right, must swim three times—in water, in butter and in wine." I agree. Michael Leny, whose father Maurice was a chef at Maxim's in Paris, first opened Cafe Society in 1987. Chef Cullen Kent, a graduate of Le Cordon Bleu in Paris, has been the owner since 2007. The two continue serving traditional European cuisine, emphasizing classic French with Belgian influences. Located in the heart of beautiful Evergreen Historic District. Banquet/Private rooms available for rehearsal dinners, wedding receptions and business functions.

Café Society

212 N. Evergreen Street Memphis, TN 722-2177 www.cafesocietymemphis.com

Belgian Cream Cake

Yield: 1 cake

Ingredients for Cake:
1 cup heavy cream
2 eggs
1 tsp vanilla
1½ cups all-purpose flour
1 cup sugar
2 tsp baking powder
½ tsp salt

Ingredients for Topping:
⅓ cup butter
⅓ cup sugar
1 Tbs all-purpose flour
1 Tbs heavy cream
2 Tbs Belgian ale

Instructions:

Preheat oven to 350 degrees.

Butter a springform pan.

Prepare cake:

Sift together flour, sugar, baking powder and salt; set aside.

Whip cream until stiff peaks form, then add eggs and vanilla and mix.

Add flour mixture to mixing bowl with cream mixture; mix just to combine.

Pour batter into prepared pan.

Bake 30-35 minutes, or until cake pulls away from side of pan; remove from oven and set aside. Note: Leave oven set at 350 degrees while you prepare topping—You will need to return cake to oven for finishing.

Prepare topping:

Melt butter in a small saucepan over medium heat.

Whisk in remaining topping ingredients and bring to a boil.

Continuing to whisk, cook topping 2-3 minutes, until slightly thickened.

Pour hot topping over hot cake and spread to cover the top.

Return cake to 350 degree oven and bake about 15 minutes more, until golden brown.

Serve cake warm or cold.

Celtic Crossing is a spirited, fun destination that "celebrates and is dedicated to the spirit of Irish pioneers who have taken up home in America." Pub patrons gather to watch live soccer broadcasts, to compete in weekly trivia contests, to listen to live Celtic music on Sundays and just to hang out at the place voted "Memphis' Most Popular Pub," by readers of the Commercial Appeal. Naturally, Celtic Crossing offers a selection of stout, whiskey, beer and wine. The food choices tempt the palate as well. Let me tell you about the Scottish Eggs: handcrafted sausage and fresh, hardboiled eggs, served with thinly sliced potatoes and a Guinness Dijon dipping sauce — satisfying, toothsome fare. Customer favorites include Guinness Beef Stew, Shepherd's Pie and Fish & Chips, of course. (Fish & Chips fans take note: 2-for-1 price on Fish & Chips all day every Tuesday, dine-in only.) Less traditional menu items: Corned Beef Sliders and Mac & Cheese. Celtic Crossing is a little piece of Ireland located in the heart of Cooper-Young. Open 7 days a week.

Celtic Crossing

Guinness Beef Stew

Yield: 4 servings

Ingredients:
1 lb beef stew meat
1 medium white onion, chopped
Olive oil
3 large carrots, chopped
4 large red potatoes,
roughly chopped
1 stalk celery, chopped
Salt to taste
White pepper to
taste
1 Tbs rosemary
1 Tbs thyme
1 Tbs garlic powder
1 cup beef stock
1 cup Guinness
Water
Cornstarch

Method:

In a large pot, brown meat and onions with a little olive oil.

Reduce heat to simmer; add carrots, potatoes, celery, salt and pepper, herbs, garlic powder, stock and Guinness.

Cook at a very slow simmer, uncovered, until meat is tender. The stew should simmer so slowly that you only see a little steam and a few bubbles rising to the surface. Allow about 1½ hours of cooking time.

Add a little water to increase amount of broth.

If you prefer a thicker broth, dissolve about 1 Tbs cornstarch in a small amount of water. Add cornstarch mixture to stew and simmer for a few minutes more, until cornstarch cooks and thickens broth a bit

Scottish Eggs

Yield: 2 servings

Ingredients:
1 Tbs all-purpose flour
⅛ tsp salt
⅛ tsp ground black pepper
4 hard-cooked eggs, peeled
4 uncooked pork sausage patties
1 egg, beaten
⅔ cup dry breadcrumbs
1 qt oil for frying

Method:

In a medium bowl, combine flour, salt and pepper.

Coat each sausage patty with the flour mix.

Mold each sausage patty around one of the hard-cooked eggs, rolling between your hands to shape.

Place beaten egg and breadcrumbs in separate dishes. Dip the sausage balls into beaten egg, then roll in breadcrumbs until coated. Shake off any excess.

Heat oil in a large saucepan or deep fryer to 365 degrees F (or 180 degrees C), or until a cube of bread dropped into the oil turns brown in 1 minute.

Lower sausage covered eggs carefully into hot oil. Fry for 5 minutes, or until deep golden brown.

Serve hot or cold with your choice of dipping sauce.

Chez Philippe is the only Forbes Four-Star restaurant in the Mid-South, and perhaps the only French restaurant in the world where duck will never be offered. Chez Philippe is the signature restaurant of The Peabody Memphis, where the official hotel mallards march into and out of the opulent Peabody Grand Lobby each day on their way to and from their work: swimming in the large, travertine marble fountain.* You'll never be served duck at The Peabody, but Galettes de Crab, Peach & Foie Gras Brûlée, Sweet Corn Basil Soup, Roasted Squab Breast "with Roquefort blue cheese grits," Niman Ranch Rack of Lamb have all appeared on the seasonal menus. Every bite, every morsel is phenomenal; the seven courses are fit for royalty. My seventh course, Chocolate-Praline Napoleon, was something to write home about, by the way. The service is exemplary at this AAA Four-Diamond Award winning restaurant, which is "worth a special trip," according to The New York Times. Fabulous food in a legendary setting. Open Wednesday- Saturday nights.

Chez Philippe

The Peabody 149 Union Memphis, TN 529-4188 www.peabodymemphis.com

Galettes de Crab ("Shrimp Mousse Crab Cakes")

Yield: 4-5 crab cakes

Ingredients:
1 lb 16-20 count shrimp, shelled and deveined, tails removed, diced
2 egg whites
1 tsp kosher salt
1½ cups heavy cream
1 lb jumbo lump blue crabmeat
(pick out any remaining shells)
1 Tbs chopped tarragon
1 Tbs chopped chervil
Butter
Cooking oil

Recommended equipment:

A large oven-safe sauté pan
Four or five 3" diameter ring molds (i.e., one per crab cake)

Directions:

Part 1: Prepare shrimp mousse/crabmeat mixture:

1) Preheat oven to 400 degrees.

2) Using a food processor, purée together the diced shrimp, egg whites and salt to a very smooth consistency. Blend in the heavy cream. Season the shrimp mousse with additional salt, according to taste.

3) In a bowl, fold the tarragon and chervil into the picked crabmeat.

4) Fold the crabmeat mixture into the shrimp mousse.

Part 2: Form and cook crab cakes:

1) Butter the inside of each ring mold.

2) Fill each ring mold with mousse and crabmeat mixture.

3) Over medium flame, heat a little cooking oil in an oven-safe sauté pan: Use just enough oil to cover the bottom of the pan.

4) Transfer the crab cakes, still in the ring molds, to the hot sauté pan to cook.

Cook for 1 minute and then slide the ring molds off the crab cakes.

Continue to sauté the crab cakes until they have good color on the bottom, then flip the cakes over and brown them on the other side.

7) To finish, transfer the crab cakes (still in the oven-safe sauté pan) to the preheated 400 degree oven and bake for 4 minutes.

A bistro feel, somewhat European, a high energy, happening place. That's The Elegant Farmer. Glancing over the menu, I noticed Curry Sweet Potato Soup, which can be too sweet and rich for my taste, and decided to give it a try: wholesome, perfectly seasoned, just right. The sophisticated Sloppy Joe was awesome. Flavors ignite. A few menu items that really attracted my attention: Old School Salmon Patties, Pan Seared Mississippi Catfish, Pot Roast, Grilled Bratwurst. Sides offered include Braised Greens, Cornbread Pudding and Oven Roasted Vegetables. I went ape over the Sweet Potato Pie — delicious, with the lightest and flakiest crust. Love it! Mac Edwards, owner/chef, is a huge supporter of local producers: Neola Farms, La Baguette, McCarter Coffee, Lake Catfish Farms, Delta Pecans, Jones Orchard and many more.

The Elegant Farmer

262 S. Highland Memphis, TN 324-2221 www.theelegantfarmerrestaurant.com

Pecan Butter

Yield: About 2 cups

Ingredients:
2 cups Delta Pecan Pieces*
¼ cup Delta Blues 100% Pure Virgin Pecan Oil*

Equipment:
Sauté pan (avoid the non-stick type)
Wooden spoon or metal spatula
Shallow, heatproof container
for cooling pecans
Food processor or blender

Directions:

Heat dry sauté pan over burner
at high heat.

When pan is hot, add pecans to pan and reduce heat
immediately to medium.

Using a wooden spoon or spatula, keep the pecans
moving constantly in the pan, to prevent burned spots.

As soon as the pecans become fragrant, remove the sauté
pan from heat and transfer the pecans to the shallow,
heatproof container. Spread the pecans out in a single
layer to cool.

Place cooled pecans in processor bowl or blender
container and pulse until the pecans are just chunky.

Continuing to pulse, gradually incorporate ¼ cup pecan
oil by drizzling it in through the opening in the top of the
processor or blender.

Transfer pecan butter to an airtight container and
store in refrigerator.

Chef's Comment: We serve this Pecan Butter with
local preserves and toasted wheat bread as our
lunchtime PB&J.

*Our local source is Delta Pecan Orchard,
473 MS Hwy 3, Tutwiler MS 38963 or on the web
at www.deltapecan.com .

Sweet Potato Pie

Yield: 1 pie (8 servings)

Ingredients:
1 lb sweet potatoes
½ cup butter, softened
1 cup white sugar
½ cup milk
2 eggs
½ tsp grated nutmeg
½ tsp ground cinnamon
1 tsp vanilla extract
One 9"-inch unbaked pie crust

Directions:

1) Preheat oven to 375 degrees.

2) Roast potatoes 45-60 minutes, until very soft.

3) Cool completely, then remove peel.

4) Place the peeled sweet potatoes in a mixer bowl and
and mix to break them apart. Add softened butter and
mix well. Stir in sugar, milk, eggs, nutmeg, cinnamon and
vanilla. Beat until smooth.

5) Pour mixture into pie
crust and bake at 375
degrees for 50-60
minutes, or until
a knife inserted
into the center
comes out
clean.

6) Allow to
cool completely
before serving.

Alex Grisanti is following family tradition. Chef Alex is the son of Ronnie, nephew of John and Frank, grandson of Elfo, and great grandson of Rinaldo, all successful chefs and restaurateurs in Memphis. I know Alex's dad, a talented chef with a passion for great food; I knew his Uncle John, whose restaurant on Airways was a Memphis landmark. Alex, chef/owner of Elfo's, serves Tuscan food that Memphians love, Tuscan in the style of La Famiglia Grisanti. Alex is a certified ACF* Chef with degrees from Johnson and Wales and the Culinary Institute of America; he trained with leading chefs in Italy. My entrée of seared sea scallops on a bed of wilted spinach with purple onion, gorgonzola cream sauce, roasted tomatoes and toast points — Yummmm. FYI: Locals know to order Tuscan gravy for their garlic bread. Elfo's serves handmade pasta dishes that would win the approval of a good Italian grandmother. I want to go back ASAP for the Gorgonzola Filet: "Bacon-wrapped, Stuffed with Gorgonzola Cheese, Encrusted with Garlic and Served over a bed of Wild Mushrooms." Group orders/catering; private dining; special luncheons. Opens at 4:00 p.m. Monday-Saturday.

*American Culinary Federation

Elfo's Restaurant

2285 S. Germantown Rd. Memphis, TN 753-4017 www.elfosrestaurant.com

Spinach Uova

Yield: 8 servings

Ingredients:
1 lb frozen spinach, thawed and drained
1 cup olive oil
1 Tbs minced garlic
14 eggs
½ cup grated Pecorino cheese
Salt and pepper to taste

Directions:
Squeeze thawed and drained spinach well.
In a large saucepan, heat olive oil until hot and add the spinach.

Add minced garlic and sauté until spinach is cooked through.

In a large bowl, whisk eggs.

Stir eggs into hot spinach mixture.

Fold in Pecorino cheese.

Season to taste with salt and pepper and serve.

Chef's comments: "In cooking, I believe in true Tuscan warm-to-the-heart food, with big red wines meant to be shared with the people you love. We're the fifth generation of Grisantis, and it's about keeping my family's recipes true to the way they were written, and creating a special memory that you carry with you."

Equestria rules the roost for contemporary international cuisine in Germantown. The on-site garden is home to a flock of chickens with a crowing rooster. These chickens earn their keep, producing the ultimate in fresh eggs for Equestria. From this on-site garden complete with greenhouse, the staff harvests equally fresh herbs and vegetables. Locally farmed beef, pork, lamb and chicken, plus seafood from the Gulf and locally sourced trout are featured on the menu. Starters to whet your appetite: Fried Calamari "served with cilantro and roasted serrano aioli;" Barreled Beef, "scotch marinated and wood roasted beef served with jus onion." Soup selections: Seafood Bisque with fresh seafood; Cauliflower Soup with crème fraiche. For my entrée, I chose the Seasonal Fish Pontchartrain, made that day with trout and served with wild rice, sautéed spinach and mushrooms, lump crabmeat, and a Pontchartrain sauce. Outstanding, a trout Pontchartrain that I'd feel comfortable recommending to the most discerning of diners. Vegetarian and gluten-free options available. An extensive and well-priced wine list. Elegant and comfortable setting. Closed Sunday and Monday.

Equestria Restaurant *3165 Forest Hill-Irene Germantown, TN 869-2663 www.equestriacuisine.com*

Trout Pontchartrain

Yield: 6 servings

Part I: Pontchartrain Sauce*

Ingredients:

½ cup all-purpose flour
4 Tbs unsalted butter
1 qt shrimp or seafood stock, reduced by ⅓
1 cup heavy cream
1 cup half and half cream

½ cup Worcestershire sauce
Salt to taste
Cayenne pepper (optional)
(6 Tbs lump crabmeat, for finishing)*

Technique:

Make a blond roux with the flour and butter.

Whisk in the reduced stock, heavy cream, half and half, Worcestershire sauce and salt. (Optional: Add cayenne pepper to taste.)

Simmer, stirring occasionally, for 15-20 minutes, until sauce thickens and the raw flour taste is gone. Remove from heat and set aside*.

*Note: This sauce can be made a day ahead: Let cool to room temperature, then refrigerate until needed. Lump crabmeat will be added immediately before serving.

Part II: Trout

Ingredients:

6 trout fillets, skin on
  Blackened seasoning
    6 oz crimini mushrooms, sliced
    12 oz fresh baby spinach
    4 cloves garlic, minced
    Splash of white wine

Technique:

Season both sides of fillets with blackened seasoning.

In a lightly oiled pan or on a griddle, sear and blacken fleshy side of fish, then turn and cook through on skin side.

Meanwhile, heat a lightly oiled sauté pan to just under smoke point, then add mushrooms and cook until they brown.

Add spinach to pan with mushrooms. Wilt spinach slightly; add minced garlic and a splash of wine. Remove from heat.

Part III: Finished Dish

Additional Ingredients:
  6 Tbs lump crabmeat
  6 servings cooked wild grain rice**

Technique:

If necessary, reheat Pontchartrain Sauce; incorporate lump crabmeat.

Plate each fillet over a serving of hot rice. Spoon equal portions of Pontchartrain Sauce over fillets and serve with spinach and mushrooms.

**We plate Trout Pontchartrain over wild grain rice; white or brown rice would also work well.

For over fourteen years, Erling Jensen, The Restaurant, has been dedicated to globally inspired and classically executed cuisine featuring the highest quality seasonal ingredients. Beloved by area residents, Erling Jensen's has received favorable coverage in the local media as well as in national publications: Memphis magazine, Memphis Business Journal, Food & Wine, Southern Living, Mariani's Virtual Gourmet Newsletter. A classy, hip and intimate spot where lush bouquets of fresh roses set the tone for fine dining every evening. Recently added, Erling's Bar is a welcoming place for a special drink and delicious snacks. It's also a comfortable spot for a superb yet casual meal. Bar patrons may order from the extensive and enticing bar menu: How about Erling's Bar Burger ("Blackened Buffalo with Crispy Benton Bacon and Stilton Aioli") or Crispy Cornmeal Dusted Oysters with Lemon Caper Rémoulade? Bar patrons may also order from the full, glorious restaurant menu.

Erling Jensen
1044 S. Yates Memphis, TN 763-3700 www.ejensen.com

Rack of Lamb with Pecan, Mustard, Garlic and Molasses Crust

Yield: 2 servings

Ingredients:
26 oz (8 bone) rack of lamb
1 cup molasses
1 cup Dijon mustard
¾ cup chopped garlic
1 cup chopped pecans
Demi-glace*

Preparation:

Combine molasses, Dijon mustard and chopped garlic to make marinade.

Marinate the lamb for 8-12 hours.

Preheat oven to 400 degrees.

Remove lamb from marinade and place in roasting pan.

Roast lamb in preheated 400 degree oven until a meat thermometer inserted into the thickest part of the meat registers 135 degrees (medium rare). (Note: Cooking times vary, but you can expect roasting to take about 20 minutes.)

While lamb is cooking, warm demi-glace for serving.

Let the lamb rest for 10 minutes.

"Pack" chopped pecans on loin side of lamb and cook lamb in 400 degree oven for 2-5 minutes more, until the pecans are toasted.

Serve lamb with warm demi-glace, sweet potatoes and green beans.

*Demi-glace is a traditional French brown sauce that requires hours of preparation time. You may make your own demi-glace, of course, but in the Memphis area, you can purchase excellent demi-glace from Erling Jensen, The Restaurant.

Flight Restaurant & Wine Bar has won several prestigious awards. Flight received Wine Spectator magazine's Award of Excellence in 2010. Open Table's Diners' Choice voters (www.opentable.com) have ranked Flight among the top ten restaurants in the Memphis area, and Delta Magazine designated Flight's Shrimp & Grits as one of the 100 best dishes in the South. The menu is extensive and creative. The Grilled Pear and Camembert Salad with arugula, walnuts and vinaigrette is worthy of attention. Pork Tenderloin with parsnips, Atlantic Halibut with shrimp risotto, Ashley Farms Chicken Breast with tortellini… excellent entrée choices. By the way, almost all menu items can be ordered in "flights" of three (generous) small plates — even soups and desserts. The inviting Brodnax Room, on the second floor of the restaurant, serves as a private area for catered meetings, parties and special events. Open 7 days a week, with free valet parking.

Flight

39 S. Main Memphis, TN 521-8005 www.flightmemphis.com

Pan Seared Scallops with White Pepper Vanilla Sauce and Forest Mushrooms

Yield: 4 servings

Ingredients:

12 large scallops (size U-15 or larger), or more, if using smaller scallops
2 vanilla beans, split and scraped
2 shallots, minced
2 limes
1 cup dry white wine or champagne
White pepper
Black pepper
Salt
Sugar
1 qt heavy cream
1 lb assorted mushrooms (oyster mushrooms, shiitake, maitake, chanterelles, etc.)
½ red bell pepper, julienned (cut into matchstick size strips)
1 bunch green onions, green part only, cut into ¼-inch pieces
Cooking oil

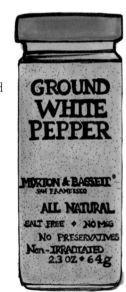

White Pepper Vanilla Sauce:

In a saucepot, heat vanilla bean pod and seeds with wine or champagne and minced shallots until liquid is reduced to ¼ cup. Add cream, juice of 1 lime, ¾ teaspoon white pepper, 1 teaspoon sugar and ½ teaspoon salt. Reduce liquid to about 1 cup. Adjust salt, sugar and white pepper to taste. Strain sauce though a fine sieve. Set aside and keep warm.

Tip: While the sauce cooks, warm the 4 plates you will use for serving this dish. Allow about 10 minutes in a warm spot.

Forest Mushrooms:

If the mushrooms are large, slice them or cut them into bite-size pieces. Sauté in a small amount of oil for about 3 minutes, or until tender. Add red bell pepper and sauté 1 minute more. Add juice of 1 lime, plus salt and pepper to taste. Add green onions and toss. Set aside and keep warm.

Note: This is a quick sauté and can be done while the scallops are cooking, if your ingredients are prepared ahead.

Pan Seared Scallops:

Heat a sauté pan large enough to hold scallops without crowding. Season scallops with salt and black pepper. When pan is very hot, add enough oil to coat the bottom of the pan. Add scallops to pan and sauté for about 2 minutes on each side, or just until the scallops are golden brown on the outside but still translucent in the center. Do not overcook.

Note: Do not disturb the scallops while cooking, except to turn them, or you will lose the crust. Exact cooking time will be determined by the size of the scallops you are using.

To Plate:

Onto the center of each warm plate, spoon a mound of mushrooms. Around each mound of mushrooms, ladle a portion of sauce. Arrange scallops on sauce, 3 per plate (or more, if you are using small scallops).

High expectations? No problem. Folk's Folly will excite you, impress you and please you. Folk's Folly serves the "Best Steak" in town, according to annual polls conducted by Memphis magazine (The city magazine nationally acclaimed for "General Excellence" with 35+ years of success in covering the Bluff City). Folk's Folly offers more than steak: Just thinking about the Australian Rack of Lamb makes me hungry. The restaurant caters to seafood lovers, as well, with high quality seafood entrées, including fresh broiled or steamed Maine lobster*. Among the appetizers, the Famous Fried Dill Pickles and Folly's Tidbits are very popular. The extensive wine list (over 250 fine wines) has received Wine Spectator magazine's "Award of Excellence" ever since 1999. (Please note: Folk's Folly has received many awards since it opened in 1977, too many for me to list here.) Live professional entertainment: Charlotte at the grand piano, Monday through Thursday evenings; Larry on Friday and Saturday evenings.* Live Maine lobsters are offered on a limited availability to ensure absolute freshness."

Folk's Folly Prime Steak House

551 S. Mendenhall Memphis, TN 762-8200 www.folksfolly.com

Folk's Folly She-Crab Soup

Yield: Eight 8-oz servings

Ingredients:
5 oz lump crabmeat
2 ½ cups heavy cream
2 minced garlic cloves
3 cups crab stock (our recipe follows) or substitute*
3 Tbs butter
3 Tbs flour
¼ cup dry sherry
Parsley to garnish

Directions for Soup:

In a large soup pot over low heat, melt butter and sauté minced garlic.

Stirring constantly, add flour and cook to make a light brown roux.

Stir in crab stock and heavy cream; bring to a boil and simmer until well blended.

Stir in lump crabmeat, reduce heat and simmer for 10 minutes.

Remove soup from heat and add dry sherry.

To serve:

Serve garnished with parsley.

Crab Stock

Yield: 2-3 quarts stock

Ingredients:
4-6 cups crab shells
½ cup dry white wine
1 large yellow onion, sliced or chopped
1 carrot, roughly sliced or chopped
2 sprigs thyme
Several sprigs parsley
1 bay leaf
10-15 whole peppercorns
2 tsp salt
Water

Directions:

Preheat oven to 400 degrees.

Place crab shells in a large roasting pan and roast in oven for 10 minutes.

Transfer roasted shells to a large stockpot; add water to cover shells, plus one inch (but no more than one inch).

On medium high, slowly heat the shells in the water until tiny bubbles appear.

Reduce heat to medium. Do not let the water boil: Maintain just below a simmer.

Do not stir the shells. Skimming the foam occasionally, let the shells cook about an hour.

Place the thyme, bay leaf and parsley in cheesecloth; secure cheesecloth with kitchen string to make a *bouquet garni*.

Add wine, onions, carrots, celery, *bouquet garni* and peppercorns. Reduce heat and maintain a low simmer for 30 minutes.

Strain stock through a fine mesh strainer; discard solids.

Use stock right away, or cool and freeze for future use.

*Concentrated seafood stock, available in many supermarkets and specialty food stores, may be substituted for the homemade crab stock.

Folk's Folly Garlic Potato Casserole

Yield: 6-8 servings

Ingredients:
4 large Idaho potatoes, washed and peeled
1 ½ qts heavy cream
¾ cup chopped garlic
4 Tbs salt
4 Tbs white pepper
2 cups Parmesan cheese
Chopped fresh parsley for garnish

1) Preheat oven to 325 degrees.

2) In a heavy saucepan, combine heavy cream, garlic, salt and pepper. Bring to a boil over medium heat. Immediately remove from heat and set aside.

3) Cut potatoes into ⅛-inch thick slices.

4) Into a greased 13" X 9" baking dish, pour a third of the warm cream mixture.

5) Overlapping the potato slices slightly, arrange half of the slices in concentric circles in the baking dish, on top of the cream.

6) Drizzle half of the remaining cream mixture over this first layer of potatoes.

7) Again overlapping the slices and arranging them in concentric circles, add the remaining potatoes to form a second layer.

8) Top potatoes with remaining cream mixture; sprinkle with Parmesan cheese.

9) Bake in preheated 325 degree oven for 45-50 minutes, until the potatoes are bubbling and golden brown.

11) Garnish with parsley and serve.

Fratelli's in the Garden has won the hearts of local foodies. Proprietor/Chef Sabine Baltz has been at the helm for 9 years and counting. Sabine's culinary skills drew my attention (and that of many others) back when Fratelli's was on the trolley line in downtown Memphis. Now operating inside the Goldsmith Garden Center at Memphis Botanic Garden, the Fratelli's menu is much more extensive. Soups are sensational. Fratelli's menu offers 19 different hot panini and 10 cold focaccia sandwiches. My favorite sandwich in the whole world is Fratelli's Porcheria: Pork tenderloin, bacon, stewed apples and spicy chipotle mayonnaise." Let me direct your attention to the Pork Tenderloin Salad, too: "Pork tenderloin, avocado, orange, spinach, roasted red peppers and spicy orange aioli." The dessert specials are always worth asking about. Goldsmith Garden Center provides an idyllic setting for a peaceful lunch. Lunch only, Monday through Saturday; Sunday lunches also, fall through spring.

Fratelli's

750 Cherry Rd. Memphis, TN 766-9900 www.fratellisfinecatering.com

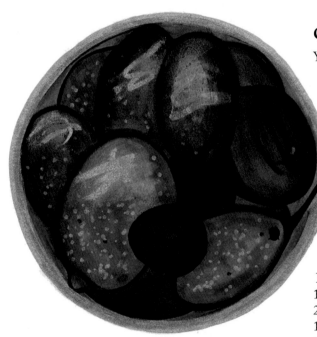

Chilled Avocado Soup

Yield: About 1 quart of soup

Ingredients:
3 whole fresh avocados
1 bundle cilantro, washed
1 large container (32 oz) plain yogurt
2 Tbs vegetable base

Preparation:

Purée ingredients together. Chill and serve.

Spicy Tomato Soup with Gorgonzola

Yield: About 3 quarts of soup

Ingredients:
1 #10 can (96 fl oz) peeled San Marzano tomatoes
2 Tbs vegetable base
1 bundle cilantro, washed
1 chipotle pepper
Gorgonzola cheese to taste

Preparation:

Purée ingredients together. Warm and serve.

First things first: I'd like to direct your attention to the Kansas City 16 oz Bone-In Filet "Served with Maître d' Butter & Cabernet Reduction" on the Grill 83 dinner menu. It's outstanding, and I'm here to spread the good word. The Kansas City filet is one very fine item among the many delicious offerings at Grill 83. For breakfast, I had smoked apple bacon and a perfect bran muffin. The Memphis Barbeque Benedict, a weekend brunch item, might be named a City of Memphis Treasure, if we gave out such awards. For lunch, I tried the Eggplant Parmesan and declared it melt-in-your-mouth good. The Chopped Salad with "Romaine, Tomatoes, Onion, Corn, Bacon, Blue Cheese, Apple and Champagne Vinaigrette" is excellent. A variety of desserts "Made Fresh Daily in the Madison's Bakery" drew and held my attention: Bourbon Pecan Pie, Dark Chocolate Mousse Torte and Warm Blackberry Bread Pudding. Yummmmm, and I'm cutting my list short at three. So many desserts, so little time. Breakfasts, brunches, lunches, afternoon tea, happy hour and dinner: Grill 83 at the jazzy, luxurious Madison Hotel serves delightful food most hours of the day, 7 days a week.

Grill 83 ~

83 Madison Ave. Memphis, TN 333-1224 www.grill83.com

Honey-Chipotle Glazed Jumbo Shrimp, Served on Sweet Corn Pudding

Yield: 8 servings

Part I: Prepare Sweet Corn Pudding

Ingredients:
1 lb fresh corn kernels
(about 4 cups)
1 small onion, chopped
1 Tbs minced garlic
1 oz sugar
1 pt cream
4 eggs
Breadcrumbs and butter as needed

Method:

In a large saucepan over medium heat, sweat corn kernels, chopped onion and minced garlic until soft. Add sugar and cream; reduce by half. Allow to cool to room temperature.

Transfer cooled mixture to food processor container. Add eggs and pulse 5 or 6 times, until corn kernels are roughly chopped.

Pour pudding into 8 mini cast iron pans or molds.

Top with breadcrumbs and a touch of butter.

Set oven to preheat to 350 degrees.

Set puddings aside while oven preheats and you prepare sauce.

Part II: Prepare Honey-Chipotle Glaze

Ingredients:
1 cup honey
2 oz chipotle peppers canned in adobo sauce
Juice of 2 limes
1 bunch cilantro, leaves and stems separated
½ oz butter (to be added at serving time)

Method:

Heat honey, chipotles, lime juice and cilantro stems together over low-medium heat for 10 minutes. Cool for 15 minutes. Strain and discard solids.

Chop cilantro leaves and place in small bowl.

Set aside ½ oz butter, chopped cilantro and strained sauce; continue to Part III.

Part III: Prepare Shrimp and Finish Dish

Ingredients:
2 Tbs vegetable oil
24 jumbo shrimp, peeled and deveined (about 2 lbs)
Salt and pepper

Method:

Bake the puddings in preheated 350-degree oven for 15 minutes, while you prepare the shrimp.

Heat a large sauté pan over high heat.

Season shrimp with salt and pepper.

Add shrimp to hot pan and sauté for 5-7 minutes, tossing shrimp every 2 minutes.

Add strained Honey-Chipotle Glaze to pan and cook 1 more minute.

Add chopped cilantro and stir. Turn off heat.

To Plate:

Place one pudding on each plate; top each pudding with 3 shrimp.

If necessary, reheat sauce; stir in ½ oz butter.

Pour an equal amount of Honey-Chipotle Glaze over each serving.

Since opening in 2004, The Grove Grill has kept up its momentum. A high percentage of diners are local, loyal customers who dine here often, my parents among them. Friday nights, after art openings at David Lusk Gallery, many gallery-goers hightail it down the sidewalk to The Grove Grill for an excellent dinner. The Grill offers delicious food in a welcoming, relaxed atmosphere. I began my meal with Rosemary Skewered Chicken Livers with onion confiture… a scrumptious starter. Next, I chose the Soup of the Day, a wonderful, perfectly seasoned oyster and artichoke soup that regular customers swear by. Among the entrées, the folks at The Grove Grill ("Home of the Best Shrimp and Grits in Memphis") are justifiably proud of their Low Country Shrimp and Grits made with Tennessee white stone ground grits and served with herb tasso gravy. Simply perfect. The Rotisserie Chicken, with "Yukon gold mashed potatoes, turnip greens and sweet garlic jus" — Southern comfort food that will put a smile on your face. For a soul satisfying dessert, go for the Warm Chocolate Cake "with Chocolate-Mint gelato." Quite a wine selection with 50+ by the glass and 100+ by the bottle.

Grove Grill
4550 Poplar Memphis, TN 818-9951 www.thegrovegrill.com

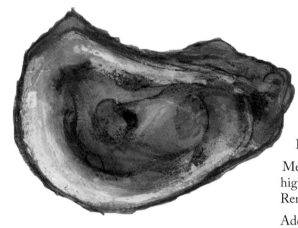

Oyster & Artichoke Soup

Yield: 8 servings

Ingredients:
¼ cup whole butter
3 slices smoked bacon
1 cup diced onion
¼ cup diced celery
1 large leek, white portion only, diced (about 1 oz)
1 cup flour
3 cups chicken stock
1 container (10 oz) fresh oysters
1 can (about 14 oz) 7-9 count artichoke bottoms, rinsed well
1 cup heavy cream

1 tsp Cajun seasoning*
Salt and pepper to taste
Several Tbs of chopped fresh basil
Oyster crackers

Directions:

Melt butter in a heavy bottomed saucepan at medium high heat. Slice bacon into ¼" pieces and add to pan. Render bacon.

Add diced onion, celery and leek to pan with bacon. Sauté the vegetables and bacon together for 3-4 minutes.

Add flour and stir to incorporate. Add stock and stir well to prevent lumps. Turn heat down to medium.

Reserving liquid, drain oysters.

Set aside 8 oysters for garnish.

Add reserved oyster liquid and remaining oysters to soup.

Reserve 2 artichoke bottoms; set aside for use in purée for garnish.

Rough chop the 5 or so remaining artichoke bottoms and add to soup.

Whisk the soup steadily to prevent flour buildup on the bottom of the pan; cook for 15 minutes.

Using a handheld blender, purée the soup.

Stir in heavy cream and Cajun seasoning; add salt and pepper to taste.

Prepare purée for garnish: Place the 2 reserved artichoke bottoms and 1 Tbs fresh basil in a food processor and purée until smooth.

To serve:

Ladle soup into 8 soup bowls. Garnish each serving with 1 whole oyster, a few oyster crackers, a little artichoke purée and some fresh basil.

*Prepared Cajun seasoning mixes are sold in many grocery stores.

This upscale restaurant continues to wine and dine the neighborhood folks and other guests. What started as an interim arrangement worked out so well that it's now permanent: Interim Restaurant & Bar is here to stay. The menu changes frequently, to take advantage of the very freshest local products and seasonal items. Always on the menu, though, is Interim's delectable Macaroni & Cheese Casserole. Sure, you can get mac & cheese casserole everywhere these days, but not made with Tripp country ham. Interim's version of mac & cheese deserves a cult following. An awesome brunch every Sunday from 10:30 a.m.–2:00 p.m. includes Braised Pork Hash and top-notch Fried Delta Catfish. Notice the white tablecloths with fresh flowers on every table — It doesn't hurt to have a fabulous florist, The Garden District, just a few doors down. By the way, the bar at Interim is in vogue as a place to see and be seen. It's also a perfect place to dine when alone.

Interim Restaurant and Bar

5040 Sanderlin, Suite 105 Memphis, TN 818-0821 www.interimrestaurant.com

Macaroni & Cheese Casserole with Tripp Country Ham* and Herb-Parmesan Crust

Yield: about 6 servings
Ingredients:
1 lb macaroni
Béchamel sauce:
4 Tbs butter (2 oz)
½ cup flour
½ gallon milk
Salt and pepper
to taste
Cheese blend:
   10 Tbs Parmesan
(about ⅔ cup),
   1 cup plus 3 Tbs
white cheddar
1 cup plus
3 Tbs Fontina
4 oz diced
country ham*
1 Tbs chopped fresh thyme
Herb-Parmesan topping:
   1 cup panko**
   ½ cup grated Parmesan
4 Tbs butter (2 oz)
1 Tbs chopped fresh thyme
1 Tbs chopped Italian parsley

Directions:

Preheat oven to 450 degrees.

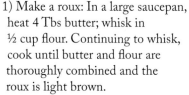

Cook the macaroni:
1) Bring a large pot of water to a boil and add a handful of salt.
2) Add the pasta and cook until fully done, about 9 minutes. Do not worry about cooking it al dente.
3) Drain pasta, then cool by rinsing with cold water.

Make Béchamel sauce:

1) Make a roux: In a large saucepan, heat 4 Tbs butter; whisk in ½ cup flour. Continuing to whisk, cook until butter and flour are thoroughly combined and the roux is light brown.
2) Whisk in ½ gallon of milk. Whisking occasionally, simmer sauce about 30 minutes. (Note: Béchamel will cook down to about 2 cups.) Season to taste with salt and pepper.

Prepare cheese blend:
In a bowl, stir together 10 Tbs Parmesan, 1 cup plus 3 Tbs white cheddar and 1 cup plus 3 Tbs Fontina to make the cheese blend.

In a small pan, sauté the diced country ham for 1 minute.

Prepare topping:
1) Melt remaining 4 Tbs butter.
2) In a small bowl, stir together the melted butter, 1 cup panko, ½ cup grated Parmesan, 1 Tbs thyme and 1 Tbs Italian parsley.

Assemble casserole:
1) In a large pot, stir together macaroni, Béchamel and cheese blend. Warm mixture over medium heat until cheese is totally melted. (Note: If the mixture is too thick, add a touch of water.) Stir in diced ham and 1 Tbs fresh thyme. Season to taste with salt and pepper.
2) Transfer the macaroni mixture to a small casserole dish and sprinkle with the herb-Parmesan panko topping.

Bake casserole in preheated 450 degree oven until top is golden brown. Enjoy!

*At Interim, we use ham from Tripp Country Hams in Brownsville, TN (www.countryhams.com).

** "Panko" is a type of flaky breadcrumb commonly used in Japanese cuisine. In the U.S., panko is sold in Asian specialty food markets as well as in many large supermarkets.

Go way up the back staircase, all the way to the 3rd floor of B.B. King's Blues Club, Memphis, and you'll discover Itta Bena Restaurant. Magical, romantic and jazzy. The menu focuses on contemporary Southern cuisine with a Delta influence. The fried avocado stuffed with crabmeat salad is so good I want to "Go tell it on the mountain, over the hills and everywhere…" One very popular dish is Duck and Waffles: "Confit of Maple Leaf Farm duck, wild rice waffles, smoked barbecue bacon dressing." A Specialty of the House: "Wild mushroom rice pilaf waffles brushed with chipotle butter, topped generously with crispy roast duck confit and finished with a blueberry-hoisin reduction, " garnished with sweet potato crisps. Desserts are Southern favorites with a French accent: crème brulée, pot de crème with wild berry compôte, bread pudding. Itta Bena could be one of Memphis' best kept dining secrets. Live vocal music Wednesday–Sunday. Subdued lighting with candles on every table. Bar seating; private dining; accommodations for large parties/special events.

Itta Bena

145 Beale Street Memphis, TN 578-3031 www.bbkingclubs.com

Crab Cakes

Yield: 4 cakes, about 4 oz each

Chef's Comments: Itta Bena serves this very traditional crab cake as an appetizer or as the main ingredient in our Crab Cake Niçoise Salad.

Ingredients:
1 lb canned crabmeat (claw meat or a combination of claw meat and jumbo lump)
1 tsp seasoned salt
2 whole eggs
2 tsp Worcestershire sauce
½ tsp dry mustard
1 tsp fresh lemon juice
2 tsp prepared Dijon (or whole grain) mustard
2 tsp melted butter
1 Tbs finely chopped parsley
1 cup prepared breadcrumbs, divided in half
For cooking: 1 Tbs oil and 1 Tbs butter
For serving: rémoulade sauce, chopped parsley and lemon wedges

Instructions:

Combine crabmeat, seasoned salt, eggs, Worcestershire sauce, dry mustard, Dijon mustard, melted butter and chopped parsley in a large bowl.

Mix gently (using your fingers is best) to avoid breaking up the crabmeat excessively.

Once these ingredients are combined, add ½ cup of the prepared breadcrumbs and incorporate into mixture.

Divide mixture into 4 equal portions and form 4 patties. Chill patties until needed.

When you are ready to cook, preheat oven to 350 degrees.

Heat a sauté pan over medium high heat. Add 1 Tbs oil and 1 Tbs butter to pan and heat until butter stops foaming. Lower heat.

Roll prepared crab cakes one at a time in remaining ½ cup of breadcrumbs, to coat.

Sauté cakes in oil and butter mixture over medium heat until golden brown on both sides, turning as needed.

Once the crab cakes are golden brown, transfer them to an ovenproof dish and bake until heated through (allow about 10 minutes).

Keep the crab cakes warm until you are ready to serve.

Serve with traditional rémoulade sauce, additional chopped parsley and lemon wedges.

Mozzarella Pimento Cheese

Yield: About 2½ cups
Chef's Comments: This is a delightful twist on the Southern tradition of pimento cheese that pairs very well with sliced summer tomatoes, crisp bacon and a simple balsamic vinegar dressing.

Ingredients:
2 cups fresh mozzarella cheese, grated
½ cup best mayonnaise, such as Hellmann's®

½ tsp seasoned salt
1 tsp finely grated sweet onion
3 Tbs roasted red peppers, drained and finely chopped, patted dry
3 Tbs finely minced fresh basil, leaves only
Fresh ground black pepper to taste

Instructions:

Gently combine all ingredients in bowl.

Chill until needed.

Serving Suggestion:

Serve one spoonful on slices of fresh tomato. Garnish with crumbled cooked bacon. Drizzle lightly with aged balsamic vinegar and best quality olive oil. Garnish with additional chopped fresh basil, according to taste. Serve with toasted French bread slices or old-school saltines.

Jim's Place ∾ *518 Perkins Ext. Memphis, TN 766-2030 www.jimsplacememphis.com*

Asparagus Salad

Yield: 8 servings

Ingredients:
1 8-oz can asparagus
(Note: You will
use both asparagus
and juice.)
6 oz cream cheese
1 ⅓ cups mayonnaise
7 oz Lemon Jell-O
Gelatin Dessert
2 cups boiling water
2 tsp almond extract (Measure precisely!)
1 cup sliced almonds

Instructions:

Drain asparagus over a mixing bowl, reserving juice in bowl.

Whip together asparagus juice and cream cheese.

Mash asparagus well.

Incorporate mashed asparagus and mayonnaise into cream cheese mixture; set aside.

Dissolve Lemon Jell-O in 2 cups boiling water; let cool to room temperature.

Add room temperature Jell-O to cream cheese/asparagus mixture and mix well.

Stir in almond extract and sliced almonds.

Refrigerate until firm.

Serve chilled.

Yellow Squash Casserole

Yield: 6-8 servings

Ingredients:
8 medium yellow squash, cut into 1-inch thick slices
1 Tbs butter
1 onion, chopped
2 Tbs canned tomato sauce
¾ cup feta cheese, crumbled
3 Tbs cracker meal crumbs
2 well beaten eggs
Salt and pepper to taste
Additional butter

Instructions:

1) Set oven to preheat to 350 degrees.

2) Cook sliced squash in boiling salted water until tender; drain well and set aside.

3) Melt 1 Tbs butter in saucepan; add onions and sauté until onions are lightly browned.

4) Add 2 Tbs tomato sauce to onions.

5) Remove saucepan from heat and add cooked squash, ½ cup crumbled feta cheese and 1 Tbs cracker meal crumbs.

6) Fold beaten eggs into squash mixture; season with salt and pepper.

7) Transfer squash mixture to greased 8" casserole.

8) Sprinkle squash mixture with remaining ¼ cup feta cheese and 2 Tbs cracker meal crumbs, then dot with additional butter.

9) Place casserole dish in a bain marie (a shallow pan of hot water).

10) Transfer casserole in bain marie to preheated 350 degree oven; bake for about 30 minutes.

Serve casserole immediately.

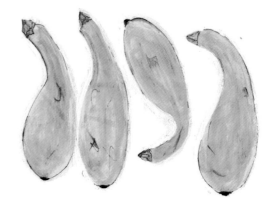

Note: This casserole freezes well: Complete casserole through step 8, then let cool to room temperature; cover tightly with aluminum foil and freeze. Allow casserole to thaw completely before continuing to steps 9 and 10.

Just For Lunch

"Now that's a real chicken salad," said Julia Child. The late, great Julia had just tasted chicken salad made by Chef Ann Barnes. Ann's cooking style is Southern with a French education. Chef Barnes serves fresh, delicious food that pleases the Ladies Who Lunch, as well as the gentlemen who know where to get a tasty mid-day meal. I'm partial to the Shrimp Ravigote in Avocado, "Shrimp salad with capers and horseradish in an avocado half," served with a delightful array of fresh breads. The Fried Oyster Sandwich, served on grilled ciabatta with rémoulade, is a Southern classic. Changing daily: Soup of the Day, Quiche of the Day, Grilled Fish… and Southern Vegetable Plate. BLT with avocado on ciabatta with red peppers and pesto mayonnaise, EVERY day! (Some things don't need to change.) Just for Lunch offers top-notch catering. When you get a chance, try Ann's lamb chops: stuffed with couscous and served with a red wine zinfandel sauce. I tasted these at a party. Whoa, I went back for more, and more. I'm not shy. Chef Barnes' charming European style tearoom is located in Chickasaw Oaks Village on Poplar. .

Creole Eggs

Yield: 6 servings

Chef's Comment: "This is a wonderful brunch item."

Grits

Ingredients:

3 cups Delta Grind or other non-instant grits
6 cups water
¼ stick butter (the real stuff)
1 cup chopped andouille sausage
½ cup shredded white sharp cheddar cheese
1 egg

Directions:
Prepare cooked grits mixture in advance:
 1) Following directions on package of grits, cook
3 cups grits in 6 cups water.
 2) Remove grits from heat. Stir in butter, andouille sausage and cheddar cheese.
 3) Allow mixture to cool slightly, then add the egg and stir well.
 4) Transfer mixture to a shallow pan and chill thoroughly.

Cut cold grits into 6 rounds, each about the size of an English muffin.

Just before serving time, heat grits rounds in the oven (as we do at Just for Lunch) or pan fry them; serve hot.

Creole Sauce

Ingredients:

3 Tbs unsalted butter
1¼ cup finely chopped onions
1 cup finely chopped green pepper
2 ribs celery, thinly sliced
3 cloves garlic, chopped
2 bay leaves
2 cups chopped tomatoes
1¼ cup tomato juice
1 Tbs Worcestershire sauce
1 Tbs Tabasco® Sauce
2 tsp cornstarch
¼ cup water

Directions:

In a skillet, melt butter and sauté onions, green pepper, celery and garlic. Add bay leaves, then add tomatoes, tomato juice, Worcestershire and Tabasco®. Simmer until the mixture cooks down a bit.

Add the cornstarch to ¼ cup water and stir until smooth. Stir this mixture into the simmering sauce and continue to cook until the sauce thickens. Set aside and keep warm.

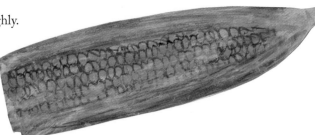

Poached Eggs

Poach 12 eggs (you know how!). Drain well.

To plate:

Place 2 warm poached eggs on a round of hot grits. Top with Creole Sauce. Yum!

Easy Corn Pudding

Yield: 4 servings

Ingredients:
 1 stick butter
 ¼ cup flour
 1 tsp salt
 1½ Tbs sugar
 1¾ cups milk (or you may use half cream and half milk)
 3 cups fresh corn, chopped*
3 eggs
Additional butter for preparing casserole
Warm water

Directions:
Preheat oven to 350 degrees.
In a medium saucepan, melt butter. Stir in flour, salt and sugar and cook until bubbly.

Stir in milk. Continuing to stir, cook until thick.

Stir in the chopped corn*.

In a small bowl, beat the eggs until frothy.

Add the beaten eggs to the corn mixture and stir to incorporate.

Generously butter a casserole.

Pour the pudding into the buttered casserole.

Set the buttered casserole inside a larger shallow pan or baking dish.

To the larger pan or dish, add about an inch of warm water, creating a bain marie.

Transfer the casserole in the bain marie to the preheated 350 degree oven. Bake for 45 minutes, or until the pudding is set.

*Whole corn may be substituted, but chopped corn makes a smoother pudding.

Pepe and Jonathan Magallanes of Las Tortugas are passionate about authentic, very fresh Mexican food. The father and son team shop daily for the freshest vegetables, fruit, meat and fish. If you lived in an upscale Mexico City neighborhood, then Las Tortugas could be your neighborhood "torteria" or "taqueria," where busy people stop for sandwiches or tacos and 100% natural fruit drinks. But Las Tortugas is on Germantown Parkway, amigos. Folks who live and/or work in the Germantown area discovered Las Tortugas a while back; the place fairly buzzes with activity at lunchtime. Midtowners have even been known to grab their passports and travel the distance, just for the fantastic fresh fish tacos, rated best in the Memphis area by enthusiasts. Tortugas, tostadas and flautas... delectable. Pepe and Jonathan themselves greet customers and take orders. Got questions? Just ask. Food is cooked to order by the efficient kitchen staff. If you're in a hurry and would like takeout, phone ahead and your takeout order will be prepared in advance for quick pickup at the counter. Open 10:30 a.m. to 8:00 p.m. Monday through Saturday.

Smoked Tinga Chicken Tostadas

This popular dish is forgiving in terms of exact proportions: Season and garnish according to preference. Enjoy!

Yield: 10-12 tostadas

(FYI: For this recipe, you will be using the breast meat from one whole chicken. One 5-lb whole, raw chicken should yield enough cooked breast meat @ about 2 oz per tostada for 10-12 tostadas.)

Ingredients:
Roasted Chicken (recipe follows)
Salsa (recipe follows)
Finely sliced white onions
10-12 fried whole corn tortillas

Garnishes:
Fresh sliced avocados
Cotija cheese
Pico de gallo sauce
Shredded lettuce
Crema fresca
Lime slices
Salt to taste

Instructions:

Skin the Roasted Chicken.

Remove all breast meat. (Refrigerate or freeze remainder of chicken for use in another dish.)

Using 2 forks, shred breast meat VERY finely.

To skillet containing prepared Salsa, add pulled chicken meat and stir to incorporate.

Add finely sliced white onions to skillet; simmer 5-10 minutes more. Avoid letting sauce get too thick.

Serve the chicken mixture evenly divided over 10-12 fried whole corn tortillas.

Garnish each tostada with avocado slices, crumbled or grated Cotija cheese, pico de gallo sauce, shredded lettuce, crema fresca and lime slices; salt to taste.

Salsa

Ingredients:
3 large tomatoes

1 clove garlic
1 small white onion
1 jalapeño pepper
2 chipotle peppers in adobo sauce
½ cup chicken stock, infused with bay and avocado leaves and strained
1 Tbs canola oil
Dash of salt

Instructions:

In an ungreased, heavy skillet over medium high heat, char tomatoes, garlic, onion, jalapeño and chipotles in adobo, turning them frequently until they are nicely blackened.

Remove and discard SOME of the large charred pieces of skin, leaving some charred pieces for smoky flavor.

Transfer charred vegetable mixture to blender container along with chicken stock and blend until smooth.

Transfer sauce from blender container to skillet. Add 1 Tbs canola oil and a dash of salt; simmer for 10 minutes. Remove from heat and set aside.

Roasted Chicken

Ingredients:

1 large, organic, whole chicken (5 lbs or larger)

Seasoning mixture: crushed chile de árbol, Mexican oregano, salt, pepper, thyme, crushed garlic, chopped shallots

Instructions:

Wash chicken and rub with seasoning mixture.

Roast seasoned chicken in oven at a temperature and for a time proportional to its size, until internal temperature reaches 190 degrees. (A 5-lb chicken would typically require about 2 hours roasting time in a preheated 375 degree oven.)

Set chicken aside to cool.

Joe and Hanh Bach, owners/chefs of Lotus, are the hardest working couple I know. They prepare everything themselves; the fresh herbs come from their own garden. I had the great good luck to discover Lotus some 25 years ago. Not too much has changed. As they say, if it ain't broke, don't fix it. Woven grass matting and bamboo strips cover some walls of the dining area; a large mural decorates the back wall. The feeling is cozy and homey. Lotus has many loyal patrons who dine here regularly. Every year, Lotus is voted "Best Vietnamese Restaurant" by readers of Memphis magazine. Try the Banh Xeo and you'll understand why. The Lemon Grass Chicken is heavenly — food for the gods. The Egg Foo Young that I've been enjoying since I was a child is right on, fantastic. In July, 1983, former Beatle Paul McCartney dined at the Lotus. His comment to a reporter was brief and to the point: "Excellent food"*. Paul was dining at the Lotus with Peter Townsend of The Who. Open daily for dinner. Takeout available; call in advance for quick pickup.

*Quoted in Memphis Press-Scimitar, July 19, 1983

Lotus Vietnamese Restaurant

4970 Summer Memphis, TN 682-1151

Bánh Xeo

Note: A popular Vietnamese dish, Bánh Xeo ("banh say-oh") is a crispy, golden brown crêpe with a pork and shrimp filling.

Yield: 4 servings (about 16 filled 10-inch crêpes)

Part I: Ground Pork and Shrimp Filling

Ingredients:
Oil for stir-frying*
1 medium yellow or white onion, thinly sliced
1 clove garlic, minced
¾ lb lean ground pork
¾ lb medium shrimp, peeled and deveined
Salt
Black pepper

Method:

Heat a little oil in a non-stick sauté pan.

Brown sliced onion, garlic and ground pork.

Add shrimp and season with salt and pepper.

As soon as shrimp turn pink and are opaque, remove pan from heat and set aside.

Part II: Bánh Xeo

Ingredients:
Oil for stir-frying*
12 oz rice flour (a tiny bit over 2 cups)
1 cup cornstarch
1 tsp turmeric
3½ cups water
1 cup unsweetened coconut milk**
Ground Pork and Shrimp Filling
3 cups mung bean sprouts

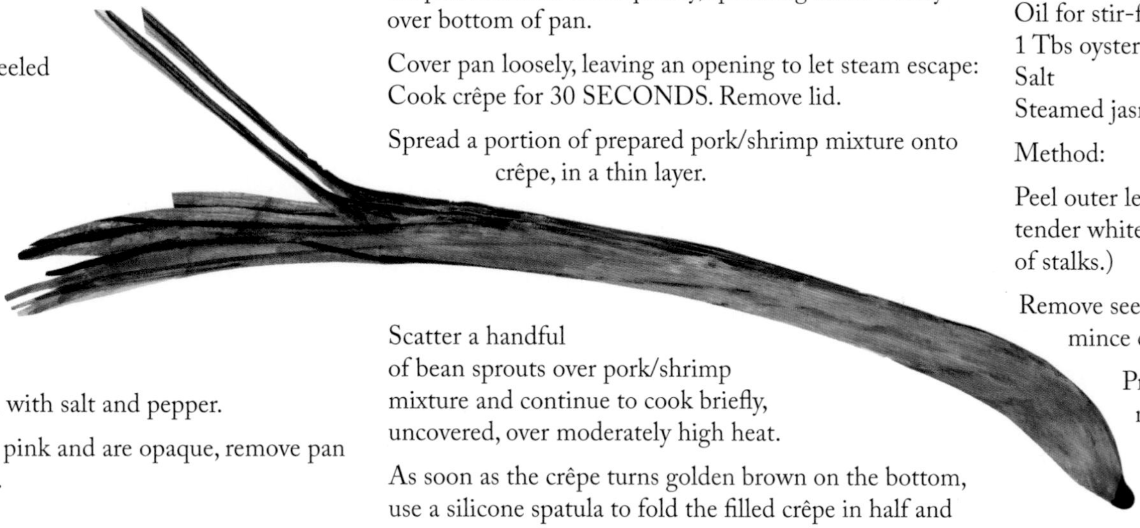

Method:

Whisk together rice flour, corn starch and turmeric with 3½ cups water and 1 cup coconut milk. Set aside for 15 minutes.

Add a little oil to a non-stick 10-inch diameter sauté pan and heat over a moderately high flame to just under the smoke point: Oil should begin to shimmer. Meanwhile, stir the batter a bit.

Pour a thin layer of batter (about ½ cup) into hot pan and tilt pan back and forth quickly, spreading batter evenly over bottom of pan.

Cover pan loosely, leaving an opening to let steam escape: Cook crêpe for 30 SECONDS. Remove lid.

Spread a portion of prepared pork/shrimp mixture onto crêpe, in a thin layer.

Scatter a handful of bean sprouts over pork/shrimp mixture and continue to cook briefly, uncovered, over moderately high heat.

As soon as the crêpe turns golden brown on the bottom, use a silicone spatula to fold the filled crêpe in half and slide it onto a plate. Serve immediately.

Repeat above steps to make each crêpe.

*Canola, peanut and grape seed oils are good choices for stir-frying.

**Stir canned coconut milk well before using.

Lemongrass Chicken

Yield: 4 servings

Ingredients:
3 stalks fresh lemongrass
2 red chile peppers
3 thinly sliced green onions
(alternative: 1 large carrot, julienned)
1 tsp sugar
1 Tbs soy sauce
1 lb skinless, boneless chicken
Oil for stir-frying*
1 Tbs oyster sauce
Salt
Steamed jasmine rice

Method:

Peel outer leaves from lemongrass stalks; mince tender white parts. (Discard outer leaves and tough parts of stalks.)

Remove seeds and stems from chile peppers and discard; mince chiles.

Prepare marinade: In a large bowl, combine minced lemongrass, minced chiles and sliced green onions. Add sugar and soy sauce. Mix well.

Cut chicken into bite-sized pieces. Transfer to bowl with lemongrass mixture; toss to mix. Cover with plastic wrap and refrigerate for 30 minutes.

Add a little oil to a large sauté pan and heat over moderately high flame until oil begins to shimmer.

Add green onions to pan and stir-fry for 2 minutes.

Add chicken mixture to pan and stir. Add oyster sauce to pan and stir-fry chicken 8-10 minutes more. Check seasoning and add salt, if needed.

Serve immediately with steamed jasmine rice.

Serving Southern influenced American entrées for more than a decade, McEwen's On Monroe is doing something right. McEwen's Chicken Pot Pie, with juicy chunks of tender white meat and happy, plump green peas, carrots, potatoes and corn, will have you singin' in the rain. With heavenly white cream sauce seasoned with a subtle mixture of herbs and spices, with light and crusty puff pastry in the middle — Best Chicken Pot Pie in America? This winter menu item has my vote. Served all year round for all you meat lovers is the Roast Beef Sandwich. The beef is piled high, topped with provolone cheese and served on a French roll with red wine jus and creamy horseradish. As for desserts, McEwen's Famous Banana Cream Pie merits continuing rave reviews. McEwen's building dates from the late 1800's. Contemporary track lighting, ceiling fans, interesting old light fixtures and salvaged architectural elements lend eclectic charm to the space. The walls are a gallery for the changing display of original works by regional artists.

McEwen's On Monroe *120 Monroe Memphis, TN 527-7085 www.mcewensonmonroe.com*

Sea Bass with Shiitake Risotto, Miso Broth and Orange Soy Glaze

Yield: 8 servings

Ingredients:
8 sea bass fillets (5-6 oz each)
Salt and pepper to taste

Directions:

Using the recipes that follow, prepare Shiitake Risotto, Miso Broth and Orange Soy Glaze. Set these aside and keep them warm.

Prepare the fish:

Season fillets with salt and pepper to taste.

In a hot skillet, pan sear until brown.

Flip fillets and pan roast for 4-5 minutes.

To plate:

In a bowl, prepare a bed of Shiitake Risotto with a little Miso Broth. Place a portion of fish on rice. Top with Orange Soy Glaze.

Shiitake Risotto
Ingredients:
2 cups Arborio rice
1 Tbs butter
¼ cup dark toasted sesame oil
1 small shallot, finely diced
1 cup steamed and julienned shiitake mushrooms
2-3 cups hot chicken stock

Directions:

In a saucepan, sauté rice with sesame oil and butter until rice is translucent.

Add diced shallot and shiitake mushrooms. Sauté until soft.

Stirring all the while, slowly add 2 cups stock and cook until rice is al dente. (Note: If rice soaks up the 2 cups of water and is not yet al dente, use additional stock to finish cooking the risotto.) Remove from direct heat. Serve warm.

Miso Broth

Ingredients:
¼ cup miso paste
1 chopped shallot
¼ cup rice wine vinegar
1 tsp chicken stock
1 tsp chopped garlic
1 tsp black pepper
1 tsp chopped ginger
4 cups water

Directions:

In a saucepan, combine all ingredients and bring to a boil. Remove from heat immediately and let cool 15 minutes. Strain to produce a clear broth; discard solids. Serve warm.

Orange Soy Glaze

Ingredients:
Juice of 4 oranges
¼ cup rice wine vinegar
1 tsp chopped garlic
1 tsp black pepper
¼ cup soy sauce
½ cup honey

Directions:

In a saucepan, combine all ingredients and bring to a simmer. Adjusting heat as needed to maintain a simmer, stir occasionally and cook until glaze thickens. Remove from direct heat. Serve warm.

Slightly rustic, dark wood paneling, lightly textured terra cotta colored walls, handsome leather upholstered benches and subdued lighting create a rural Northern California feel. Large paintings* by Memphis artist John Robinette are displayed on the walls. Artsy and relaxed, yet refined, Napa Café brings a touch of the wine country to East Memphis. The emphasis is on California wines and Napa Valley style cuisine. My artist's eye was attracted to the colorful vegetables that accompanied my entrée of lamb loin: bright green asparagus and orange, white and purple carrots. Lovely, delicious. The Lobster Bisque with Black Truffle Foam was amazing, sensually so. The Caramelized Diver Scallops with "Melted Leeks & Turnips with Rock Shrimp, Cauliflower Purée and Red Wine Gastrique" captured my heart. Memphis magazine readers chose Napa Café for their Award of Excellence for Best Atmosphere in 2010, and the wine selection has merited Wine Spectator's Award of Excellence for twelve years in a row. In short, the list of awards is long! Private dining areas, catering and takeout available.

*Paintings by John Robinette are available for sale.

Napa Cafe

5101 Sanderlin, Suite 122 Memphis, TN 683-0441 www.napacafe.com

Lobster Bisque with Truffle Foam

Yield: 12-14 servings

Ingredients for Lobster Bisque:

10 lobster bodies
2 large carrots, chopped
2 onions, chopped
4 stalks celery, chopped
3 bay leaves
1 bunch thyme
2 gallons water
2 qt heavy cream
1 cup tomato paste
Juice of 4 lemons
Salt and pepper to taste

Prepare Lobster Bisque:

Roast lobster bodies in a preheated 350 degree oven until bright red.

Add lobster bodies, carrots, onions, celery, bay leaves, thyme and water to a large pot and bring to a boil, then reduce to a simmer. Simmer stock for 1½ hours.

Strain the lobster stock and discard solids. Place strained stock back on heat and continue to simmer until stock is reduced by half.

Stir cream, tomato paste, lemon juice, salt and pepper into reduced stock.

Continue to simmer soup gently until it reaches desired consistency.

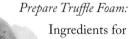

Prepare Truffle Foam:

Ingredients for
Truffle Foam:
½ qt heavy cream
4 Tbs truffle oil
1 Tbs sugar
1 Tbs salt

Combine ingredients in a mixing bowl and whisk until stiff peaks form.

To serve:

Ladle a portion of Lobster Bisque into an individual soup bowl; garnish with Truffle Foam.

Seared Scallops with Melted Leeks and Turnips, Served with Cauliflower Purée and Red Wine Reduction

Yield: 2 servings

Ingredients:
5 Tbs butter
3 turnips, peeled and diced
2 leeks, white parts only, sliced very thinly
1 cup red wine
1 cup red wine vinegar
1 cup sugar
½ head cauliflower
½ qt cream
2 sprigs thyme, leaves only
3 cloves garlic
Salt and pepper to taste
4 dry-packed sea scallops (size: 10-20 per lb)
2 Tbs vegetable oil

Prepare Melted Leeks and Turnips:

Melt 5 Tbs butter in a sauté pan over very low heat.

Add sliced leeks to pan and cook until tender. Set aside.

Blanch peeled, diced turnips in boiling water until tender; drain.

Add drained turnips to leek mixture; season to taste with salt and pepper.

Set aside and keep warm.

Prepare Red Wine Reduction:

Combine red wine, vinegar and sugar in a saucepan. Simmer until liquid is reduced by half and has the consistency of syrup. Set aside and keep warm.

Prepare Cauliflower Purée:

Combine cauliflower, cream, thyme leaves and garlic cloves in a medium sized saucepan.

Bring mixture to a boil, then reduce to a simmer.

Cook until the cauliflower is tender.

Blend cauliflower mixture until smooth. Set aside and keep warm.

Prepare Seared Scallops:

Preheat oven to 350 degrees.

Place an ovenproof sauté pan over medium high heat; add vegetable oil.

While the pan is warming up, season the scallops on both sides with salt.

Once the pan is hot, sear the scallops on both sides until golden brown.

Transfer scallops in ovenproof sauté pan to preheated 350-degree oven to cook until just firm.

Remove finished scallops from oven and serve without delay.

To Plate:

Place 2 scallops on each (warmed) dinner plate. Drizzle with Red Wine Reduction and serve with prepared vegetables.

With 37+ years of successful operation, Paulette's has established itself as a Memphis institution. Long recognized in local readers' polls for consistently high quality Continental cuisine and romantic atmosphere, Paulette's in its new location in the River Inn on Mud Island is as charming as ever. The fabulous brass chandelier from the Midtown location now hangs in the new restaurant. The décor is a bit more formal and the setting is more dramatic these days. High windows in the new location offer diners spectacular views of Downtown and the Mississippi River. The view from the 4th floor terrace is breathtaking. Loyal fans of Paulette's will be thrilled to find Hungarian Gulyas, Ham Palacsinta, Low Country Crab Cakes and Kahlua-Mocha Parfait Pie still on the menu. An appetizer to die for: Lump Crabmeat Stuffed Mushrooms. Paulette's justifiably famous Sunday brunches (11 a.m.–2 p.m.) continue: crêpes and omelettes for every taste, Roasted Beef Tenderloin Sandwich, Brioche French Toast and Sausage, Niçoise Salad and more delights. Breakfast, lunch and dinner daily. Happy hour daily, 4 p.m.–6:30 p.m. with a special bar menu. Plenty of parking space; complimentary valet parking.

Kahlúa® Mocha Parfait Pie (K-Pie)

Yield: One 10" pie (8 servings)

Ingredients:
½ cup butter
7 oz sweetened flaked coconut
½ cup finely chopped pecans
2 Tbs all-purpose flour
1 gallon coffee chocolate chip ice cream, slightly softened*
Garnishes:
Grated semisweet chocolate
½ pt cold whipping cream
1 cup original flavor Kahlúa® coffee liqueur

Preparation:

1) Preheat oven to 325 degrees.

2) In a small saucepan, melt butter completely.

3) In a large bowl, combine coconut flakes, flour and chopped pecans.

4) Add melted butter and mix well, until all dry ingredients are moistened.

5) Press coconut mixture in an even thickness over the bottom and side walls of a 10" metal pie pan. Pack crust firmly against sides and into area where sides and bottom meet. Press crust just to the top of the pie tin sides: Do not extend crust onto pie tin rim.

6) Bake crust in preheated 325 degree oven until it is golden brown.

7) Set crust aside to cool completely before filling. (Note: Crust may be prepared ahead and frozen until needed.)

8) Pack cooled crust with slightly softened coffee chocolate chip ice cream to form a large, rounded pie.

9) Cover pie with foil and refreeze.

Service:

Cut frozen K-Pie into 8 equal slices.

Using a refrigerated bowl and beaters, whip cold cream until soft peaks form.

Top each slice with 1 heaping Tbs whipped cream, semisweet chocolate shavings and a 1-oz serving of Kahlúa®.

*FYI: Ben & Jerry's has offered this flavor under the name, Coffee Heath® Bar Crunch. If commercially prepared coffee chocolate chip ice cream proves hard to find, simply incorporate a generous amount of Hershey's Heath® English Milk Chocolate Toffee Bits (available in the baking section of supermarkets) into softened coffee ice cream.

Pete & Sam's exemplifies the concept of "family restaurant." No fancy white tablecloths here — this is a no fuss place. Pete & Sam's has been serving simple, authentic Italian style home cooking for almost 60 years to Memphians of all ages. My youngest son has been a regular patron since he was 6 weeks old. He's almost 22 years old now, and his favorite restaurant is (OK, you guessed it!) Pete & Sam's. The thin crust pizzas are great. The Ravioli & Spinach & Egg entrée is always tasty. Pete & Sam's makes a delicious chicken liver dish, baked in a casserole with bell peppers, mushrooms and provolone cheese, that I've never seen offered anywhere else. The bacon wrapped filet mignon may not be strictly Italian, but it's certainly worthy of applause. You can end your meal with a classic Italian dessert: Spumoni, Cannoli, Tortini or Tiramisu.

Pete and Sam's

3886 Park Memphis, TN 458-0694 www.peteandsamsrestaurant.com

Summer Sweet Tomato Sauce

Yield: About 6 servings

Ingredients:
1 56-oz can whole peeled tomatoes (preferably the San Marzano variety)
½ bunch parsley
½ large yellow onion
⅓ cup virgin olive oil
½ cup sugar
½ cup tomato paste

Instructions:

Saving the juice in a bowl, drain the tomatoes.

Chop drained tomatoes to desired size, medium to fine. Place chopped tomatoes in bowl with juice.

Remove and discard parsley stems; mince parsley leaves.

Chop onion to medium dice.

In a stockpot over medium heat, sauté chopped onion in olive oil until tender and translucent.

Add tomatoes with juice to stockpot.

Add sugar and tomato paste to mixture and stir to incorporate.

Reduce heat and let sauce simmer for about 1½ hours, stirring occasionally.

Serve this sauce on your favorite pasta.

Chef's Comments: "This is a very easy recipe that does not require a lot of time or skill to make. Don't let the "lack of ingredients" fool you: This is a wonderful sauce! My favorite dish with this sauce is a really good variation:

"Refrigerate the sauce overnight in a large bowl. Ladle 2 cups of sauce into a separate container and set aside. To the large bowl of sauce, add ⅓ to ½ cup ricotta cheese and stir in toughly. Add your favorite spicy cooked Italian sausage. (I prefer thinly sliced sausage for this dish.) Coarsely chop several leaves of fresh sweet basil and stir in. Next, add cooked penne pasta to the bowl and stir gently to coat all the pasta with sauce. Transfer the sauce and pasta mixture to a casserole dish. Top the casserole with a thin layer of the reserved "original" sauce. Finish the casserole with ribbons of provolone cheese. Bake in a preheated oven at

350 degrees for 10-15 minutes. Sprinkle heated casserole with more chopped fresh basil and grated Parmesan cheese and serve. "

Chef Kelly English and Restaurant Iris took top honors in the 2010 annual readers' poll sponsored by Memphis *magazine: Best Restaurant, Best Chef, Best Service, Best Wine List, Best Ambience, Best Place to Impress. Also in 2010, English was named James Beard Award Semifinalist for Best Chef: Southeast. Same year, he appeared on Food Network's show, "The Best Thing I Ever Ate." Restaurant Iris serves French Creole cuisine in a charming old Midtown house. All three dining rooms are intimate, with ever-changing displays of original artwork. The "salad of Brussels sprouts" with "Allan Benton's bacon, and sherry" is a superb way to begin your meal. As a second course, "to continue," I recommend the "yellow jack, local tomatoes, shrimp and a harissa 'café au lait,'" which I sampled at a cooking demonstration in Little Rock, Arkansas. One taste of this delight, and I could see into my future: I would go to Restaurant Iris in Memphis for a whole serving. Chef Kelly English shows great passion for food and he aims to please! Open Monday-Saturday for dinner; one Sunday brunch each month. Private dining; private parties/special events.*

Restaurant Iris *2146 Monroe Memphis, TN 590-2828 www.restaurantiris.com*

"Salad" of Brussels Sprouts, Bacon and Sherry

Yield: 4 servings

Ingredients:
40 Brussels sprouts
8 slices of your favorite bacon, cut into short strips
2 shallots, minced
4 cloves garlic, minced
3 Tbs fresh thyme leaves
2 Tbs sherry vinegar
6 Tbs olive oil
Salt and pepper to taste

Clean and pick over the Brussels sprouts, removing discolored leaves and trimming away tough stems. Cut each sprout in half, lengthwise.

In a large pot, bring 1 gallon salted water (as salty as the ocean) to a rolling boil.

Fill a second large pot or bowl with ice water and set it near the stove.

Blanch the sprouts in the boiling water just until they become fork tender (but not mushy). Using a slotted spoon or sieve, quickly transfer the sprouts to the bowl of ice water to shock them. Allow the sprouts to chill in the ice water, then drain them well in a colander.

In a small bowl, whisk together the sherry vinegar and the olive oil to make a vinaigrette.

In a large sauté pan over medium heat, render the strips of bacon. As soon as the bacon begins to crisp and the fat is released into the pan, add the drained sprouts and continue to sauté.

When the sprouts begin to take on some color, add the shallots, garlic and thyme to the pan; cook until the shallots become translucent.

Dress the warm salad (still in the sauté pan) with vinaigrette. Season to taste with salt and pepper. Enjoy!

The Grisanti family has been keeping the culinary traditions of Tuscany alive in Memphis since 1909. Chef Ronnie Grisanti's Italian specialties have attracted a loyal following since the 1980's, when he opened his restaurant on Marshall Street in the original (and current) Sun Studio building. For a while, historic Beale Street was home to the restaurant. At the current location on Poplar Avenue, Chef Grisanti continues to take inspiration from treasured Italian family recipes. All the pasta is handmade. The manicotti and the tortellini are perennial favorites. The Toasted Ravioli (BEST IN THE CITY) has its own fan club. For a serious dose of comfort food, treat yourself to Elfo's Special. I am especially taken with Melanzana Tuscana, offered "loaded" or "unloaded." I prefer this incredible eggplant dish "loaded," with artichoke hearts and mushrooms. Love it! Word to the wise: Save room for dessert…chocolate cheesecake…WOW.

Chocolate Cheesecake

Yield: One 12" cake

Ingredients:
12 oz semisweet chocolate bits
2 lbs cream cheese, softened
2 cups sugar
4 eggs
3 tsp cocoa
2 tsp pure vanilla extract
2 cups sour cream
1 Chocolate Wafer Crust, chilled (recipe follows)

Recommended Equipment: One 12" springform pan with 3" sides; a kitchen mixer; a food processor, blender or rolling pin

Instructions:

Preheat oven to 350 degrees.

Melt semisweet chocolate bits in top of double boiler over warm water.

In a large mixing bowl, beat softened cream cheese until smooth.

Beating steadily, gradually add sugar to cream cheese.

Add one egg at a time to the cream cheese mixture, beating after each addition.

Add melted chocolate, cocoa and vanilla; mix thoroughly.

Fold sour cream into chocolate/cream cheese mixture.

Transfer filling to chilled crust.

Bake in preheated 350 degree oven for 1 hour 10 minutes. (Note: Cake will be slightly runny, but will become firm as it chills.)

Let cool to room temperature, then refrigerate for at least 5 hours before serving.

Chocolate Wafer Crust

Yield: Crust for one 12" cheesecake

Ingredients:
2 sticks butter
3 cups chocolate wafer crumbs*

Instructions:

Grind chocolate wafers finely in a food processor or blender, or crush manually with a rolling pin.

Melt butter.

Stir butter and crumbs together until well blended.

Press mixture evenly across the bottom and about 2¾" up the sides of a 12" diameter springform pan.

Chill crust completely before using.

*FAMOUS® Chocolate Wafers from Kraft Foods are available in most supermarkets. Finely ground, 39-40 of these wafers will make 3 cups of crumbs

Elfo's Special

Yield: 2 servings
Ingredients:
4 oz thin spaghetti
Salt
2 Tbs olive oil
2 cups butter
6 large cloves garlic, minced
6 jumbo raw shrimp, peeled and quartered
4 large mushrooms, thinly sliced
4 Tbs freshly grated Romano cheese
Freshly ground white pepper

Garnishes:
Freshly grated Romano cheese
Freshly chopped parsley

Instructions:

Place a serving dish in a 200 degree oven to warm while you cook.

Over high heat, bring a large pot of salted water to a rapid boil.

Add 2 Tbs olive oil to boiling water.

Add 4 oz thin spaghetti to pot and cook for 10 minutes, stirring to prevent noodles from sticking together.

Drain cooked spaghetti in a colander, rinse with cold water and set aside.

(Note: The next steps require you to increase the heat progressively from low to medium to high and cook without browning the butter: Keep the contents of the pan moving (Don't stop tossing!) and, if necessary, adjust the flame or lift the skillet from the burner briefly from time to time.)

In a large skillet over low heat, melt 2 cups butter.

Add minced garlic, quartered raw shrimp and sliced mushrooms; increase heat to medium and cook JUST until shrimp pieces turn pink.

Immediately add cooked spaghetti to skillet and toss to combine.

Tossing steadily, sprinkle pasta mixture with 4 Tbs Romano and season to taste with freshly ground white pepper.

Using a large spoon, turn spaghetti mixture over from edge of skillet to center, taking care not to cut spaghetti.

Turn burner to high and continue to toss and cook pasta mixture until it is very hot. Remove skillet from heat immediately.

Transfer pasta mixture to warm serving dish.

Garnish with additional freshly grated Romano cheese and freshly chopped parsley; serve immediately.

Artsy but not funky, intimate but not secluded, Sweet Grass bills itself as a neighborhood bistro serving South Carolina Low Country cuisine. After visiting my children at The College of Charleston over a period of seven years and maximizing opportunities to try the best food in Charleston, I'm an expert when it comes to shrimp and grits: Sweet Grass rules. You've heard from an expert. As good as it gets. The Fried Green Tomato BLT with Apple Wood Smoked Bacon, by the way, merits your attention. Deeee-licious. You will not leave Sweet Grass hungry. Desserts aplenty here, Deep Dish Sour Cream Apple Pie, Chocolate Peanut Butter Pie, Crème Brulée, Peach Cobbler with Vanilla Gelato. While at Sweet Grass, you might want to visit Next Door, the restaurant's latest addition. More casual, a bit more lively, Next Door is fitted out with seven ordinary flat screen TV's plus one outrageously large TV. What Chef Ryan Trimm brings to the table at Next Door is more delectable food. Dining at either place is a treat.

Sweet Grass

937 S. Cooper Memphis, TN 278-0278 www.sweetgrassmemphis.com

Roasted Butternut Squash Bisque

Yield: 8 servings
5 butternut squash, medium sized
¼ cup pork lard (vegetarian soup: substitute vegetable oil)
1 small yellow onion, peeled and chopped
3 cloves garlic
¼ cup peeled and chopped fresh ginger
2 Granny Smith apples, peeled and chopped
2 cups milk
6 cups chicken stock
(vegetarian soup: substitute water)
½ cup chopped bacon (vegetarian soup: omit bacon)
1 tsp ground nutmeg
1 tsp ground mace
1 cup heavy cream
Salt and pepper to taste
For garnish: ½ cup chopped pecans

Directions:

Preheat oven to 350 degrees.

Cut butternut squash in half lengthwise and remove seeds with a spoon.

Place squash halves cut side down on a rimmed baking sheet; add ¼ inch water to baking sheet. Bake until squash is tender to soft (allow 45-60 minutes for cooking).

Remove squash from oven and allow halves to cool, cut side up.

Scoop the meat from the squash skins; discard skins.

Heat lard (or oil) in a soup pot over medium high heat. Add chopped onion and sauté until tender. Add garlic, ginger and apples; cook until tender.

Add squash, milk, stock (or water), bacon, nutmeg and mace; stir to combine.

Simmer until volume is reduced by one-fourth.

Add cream to soup and purée with an immersion blender. Season to taste with salt and pepper.

To serve:

Ladle portions into individual bowls and garnish with chopped pecans. Enjoy!

77

78

Students and faculty at the Southern College of Optometry have something to be proud of, and that's the 20/20 Diner on the 4th floor, where Chef Kathy Katz does the cooking. Other colleges might have decent food, but the quality of Kathy's food is well beyond "decent." Monday through Friday she shows her passion for cooking, preparing wonderful homemade soups, salads, sandwiches and plate lunches. The daily specials are always a big hit. The 20/20 Diner is not just for students and faculty: Everyone is welcome. The décor is nothing fancy, but it's nice, with a lovely scenic view of the city. In the summer, Kathy sells some of her specialty items at the Memphis Farmers Market, downtown. I myself can never say "no" to Kathy's very tasty pimento cheese.

20/20 Diner

1245 Madison Ave. Memphis, TN 722-3289 www.memphisfarmersmarket.org/2020diner

Black Bean Hummus with Grilled Greek Pita

Yield: 8 servings

Black Bean Hummus

Ingredients:
1 16-oz can black beans, rinsed
1 16-oz can garbanzo beans, rinsed
½ bunch cilantro
2 oz pickled jalapeño peppers*
1 tsp ground cumin
1 tsp cayenne pepper
Juice of 2 limes
Pinch of salt
⅓ cup olive oil

Directions:

Place beans, cilantro, 2 oz of jalapeños*, some pepper juice from the can or jar, cumin, cayenne, lime juice and salt in the work bowl of your food processor. Start the processor. With the food processor running, gradually add ⅓ cup olive oil and process until smooth. Taste the hummus and adjust seasonings to preference.

*FYI, just in case you are working without a kitchen scale: If you are using chopped peppers, count a scant ½ cup as 2 oz. If the peppers are sliced, then count a generous ½ cup of peppers as 2 oz.

Grilled Greek Pita

Ingredients:
1 Greek pita (not the pocket kind)
Olive oil
Garlic powder
Onion powder
Oregano
Parsley

Directions:

Brush the Greek pita lightly with olive oil, then sprinkle with garlic powder, onion powder, oregano, and parsley. Grill until golden brown.

To serve:

Cut pita into 8 pieces and serve with Black Bean Hummus.

Vegetarian Tetrazzini Sauce

Yield: Sauce for 6-8 servings

Ingredients:
½ onion or 1 large shallot, diced
2 Tbs butter
8 oz fresh mushrooms, button or baby portabellas
3 Tbs cake flour*
1 cup dry white wine or red wine**
½ cup heavy cream (or half-and-half)***
16 oz can vegetable stock, warmed
½ cup shredded Parmesan cheese
1 tsp fresh thyme
Salt and pepper to taste

Directions:

Sauté onion in butter over medium heat for 2 minutes or until onion is translucent. Add mushrooms and sauté briefly.

Sprinkle flour onto onion, butter and mushroom mixture; cook for 1 minute to make roux.

Add wine and reduce by half, stirring frequently.

Stirring to incorporate, add warm vegetable stock in small increments until sauce reaches consistency of gravy. Stir in heavy cream (or half-and-half). Add Parmesan cheese, thyme, salt and pepper and stir well.

Chef's Comments: I like to use this sauce with pasta and cooked, diced chicken in casserole, topped with additional Parmesan cheese and baked at 350 degrees until golden brown or bubbly. This sauce can also be used for meats or for your favorite pasta with vegetables.

*I prefer to use cake flour (rather than all-purpose), for the finer texture.

**I prefer white wine for the color.

***Do not use fat free substitute in this recipe.

79

East Tapas & Drinks is the latest exciting addition to Wang's Mandarin House. Red painted walls, stained concrete floors, contemporary glass pendants over the über-sleek bar create a laid-back and stylish urban feel. The menu of small plates, pizzas and desserts changes seasonally, but at East, tapas are always TOPS! Ceviche, 3 cheese mac 'n cheese, Thai lime chicken wings, Asian sloppy Joes, Buffalo chicken pizza, green tea ice cream, banana tempura… flavorful little international treats. Next door, parent restaurant Wang's Mandarin House continues to serve what Memphians for 29 years have voted the best Chinese food in Memphis*. Wang's extensive 16-section menu even includes a section for "Health Food Selection" and a section of "Cantonese Suggestions." My entrée of Sha Cha Beef (Beef Taiwan Style) with eggplant was extraordinary. Live music, songs from West Side Story played by a very talented pianist, made the evening special. Whether you dine at East or Wang's, you'll enjoy delicious food in a very pleasant setting — and on some nights, live acoustic music, as well.

*in Memphis Flyer and Memphis: magazine reader polls

Wang's Mandarin House & East Tapas & Drinks

6069 Park Ave. Memphis, TN 767-6002 www.wangsmemphis.com

Guacamole

Yield: 2 servings

Ingredients:
1 medium avocado
¼ cup diced tomato
½ Tbs finely diced jalapeño
1½ Tbs finely diced shallots
1 Tbs finely diced white onion
½ Tbs minced garlic
½ tsp minced ginger
¼ tsp sea salt
¼ tsp white pepper
1 Tbs Key lime juice

Instructions:

Pit and peel avocado; cut into ½" chunks and set aside.

In a mixing bowl, stir together remaining ingredients.

Taking care to leave avocado chunks intact, add avocado pieces to bowl with seasoning mixture and toss gently.

Serve immediately with chips.

Hot and Sour Soup

Yield: About 2½ cups of soup

Ingredients for Soup Base:
1 7/8 cups water
1 Tbs cornstarch dissolved in 2 Tbs cold water
3½ Tbs soy sauce
½ Tbs chili oil (or season to taste)
2 Tbs sugar
Pinch MSG
¼ Tbs chicken broth powder
2 Tbs vinegar

Optional Ingredients:
1 whole egg, beaten*
Cooked chicken or pork, minced
Bamboo shoots

Instructions:

Add 1 7/8 cups water to deep saucepan and bring to boil over high heat.

To the boiling water, add all remaining ingredients for soup base.

Stir soup as it cooks and begins to thicken.

Taste soup for seasoning: Add a bit more chili oil for a spicier soup.

Stir in optional ingredients of your choice and serve.

*The raw egg will cook instantly when stirred into the hot soup base.

I would like to be more original, but I can't. The Woman's Exchange of Memphis describes its Tea Room quite well: "a treasured gem." I have been dining there for more than forty years and they have not missed a beat. Chef Rev has presided over the kitchen for almost sixteen years. To thank a friend or client, treat him or her to lunch at the Tea Room any Thursday and order the beef tenderloin. No one cooks it as well as Chef Rev. With the entrée you'll get a vegetable, a salad, a homemade yeast roll and a world class caramel brownie. Stop by for lunch any Friday and enjoy catfish like no other. The non-profit Exchange operates a retail shop where people can supplement limited incomes by selling handcrafted gifts and children's clothing: Special orders for children's clothing are accepted. Alice Bays Wunderlich, the granddaughter Jean Wunderlich and I were blessed with in July of 2011, is (and will continue to be!) a perfect model for beautiful heirloom quality dresses from the Exchange.

The Woman's Exchange Tea Room

88 Racine Memphis, TN 327-5681 www.womans-exchange.com

Buttermilk Chess Pie

As prepared by Louise Bailey

Yield: 1 pie (8 servings)

Ingredients:
3 eggs, beaten
1 cup sugar
1 tsp vanilla
6 Tbs buttermilk
¾ stick butter, melted
9-inch unbaked pie shell

Preparation:

Preheat oven to 350 degrees.

Mix together eggs, sugar, vanilla, buttermilk and butter; pour into pie shell.

Bake pie at 350 degrees for 30 minutes.

Reduce heat to 300 degrees and bake 10 minutes longer, or until pie is set.

Lacey Special

As prepared by Rev. Bailey

Yield: 8 servings

Ingredients:
½ cup chopped celery
½ cup chopped onion
4 oz canned mushrooms, drained
4 oz margarine
4 Tbs flour
1 qt chicken stock
1 ⅓ tsp salt
¼ tsp black pepper
2 Tbs chopped pimento
2 Tbs chopped parsley
4 cups cooked chicken or turkey, chopped
1 hard boiled egg, grated

Preparation:

Sauté the celery, onion and mushrooms in margarine until soft, but not brown.

Stir in flour and cook for a minute.

Add chicken stock and cook until thick.

Stir in remaining ingredients.

Serve hot over cornbread or rice.

Note: The Woman's Exchange accepts takeout orders for Louise Bailey's popular Buttermilk Chess Pie! Just call in advance to make arrangements.

Drive just a couple of hours west of Memphis to Little Rock to relax and be pampered at the beautiful Capital Hotel. Ashley's, one of the hotel restaurants, offers New American Cuisine that will please your palate. Executive Chef Lee Richardson deserves a special medal for his Heritage Pork Tenderloin and Crispy Belly with Maque Choux and Fried Okra. No surprise, though: He grew up in New Orleans and worked there with Chef John Besh. Through Ashley's and the Capital Hotel, Chef Richardson hosts Town and Country Culinary Weekend events. I was lucky enough to experience one of these culinary extravaganzas where the guest chef was Kelly English of Restaurant Iris in Memphis. Having both of these fine chefs presenting the weekend program was fantastic, almost overwhelming. Seven Stones Cabernet Sauvignon, from a limited production Napa Valley family winery, was the featured wine. Flawless. Also located in the Capital Hotel, The Capital Bar and Grill offers awesome weekly blue plate specials, yummy bar snacks such as pickled egg salad, andouille gravy and chips, spicy meat pies with buttermilk ranch dressing, and a hamburger that my husband has declared "World's Best."

Ashley's at the Capital Hotel

111 West Markham St. Little Rock, AR 501-374-7474 www.capitalhotel.com

**Smoked Trout with
Lemon-Dill Potato Salad and Grain Mustard**

Yield: 6 servings

Part I: Smoked Trout

Ingredients:
1 whole cold smoked trout*

Method:

With a very sharp knife, cut the skin away from the fillet; trim away any gray tissue and clean up the edges of the trout.

Slice each fillet in half from heat to tail, so that you end up with 4 very thin fillets.

First julienne the fillets, then cut the resulting strips meticulously into very small dice.

Set prepared trout aside and keep chilled until ready for service.

*We ourselves use and highly recommend Sunburst Cold Smoked Rainbow Trout from Sunburst Trout Farms in Canton NC (www.sunbursttrout.com, Tel (800) 673-3051 or (828) 648-3010). FYI: Smoked salmon would make a fine substitute for trout in this dish.

Part II: Potato Salad

Ingredients:
1 Idaho potato
2 Tbs lemon juice
½ cup salad oil
Pinch of salt
1 Tbs freshly
chopped dill
Zest of 1 lemon
¼ cup mayonnaise

Method:

Peel the potato, then trim it to form a perfect rectangular block.

Slice the trimmed potato into ⅛" slices; cut the slices into ⅛" dice.

In a saucepan of salted water over high heat, blanch the diced potato until just soft, then drain and shock in ice water. Drain.

Transfer the diced potato to a small bowl lined with paper towels and let dry.

Shake together the lemon juice, salad oil and salt.

In a small bowl, lightly dress the potatoes with the lemon juice mixture.

Add mayonnaise, lemon zest and dill; toss to combine.

Part III: Horseradish-Grain Mustard Vinaigrette

Ingredients:
⅓ cup white wine vinegar
1 cup neutral salad oil
1 Tbs whole grain mustard
1 tsp water
Pinch of salt
1 Tbs freshly grated horseradish

Method:

Mix ingredients in a shaker or in a small mixing bowl and set aside.

Part IV: The Finished Dish

Additional Ingredients:
1 Tbs capers
1 tsp minced red onion
1 tsp finely sliced chives
6 quail eggs

1 bag good quality potato chips, crushed
6 tufts of micro greens or small herb salads

Method:

Separate each quail egg: Set each yolk aside separately, in reserve; place all the whites in a bowl together.

To the bowl containing the egg whites, add the diced trout, capers, minced red onion and chives. Stir to combine and set aside.

Plate each serving:

1) Set a biscuit cutter in the center of a plate. Spoon 2 Tbs of potato salad into the biscuit cutter. Press mixture down firmly and evenly.

2) Top potato salad with 1 Tbs potato chip crumbs.

3) Add 2 Tbs of the trout mix to the biscuit cutter, again pressing firmly and evenly.

4) Carefully slide the biscuit cutter away.

5) Drop an egg yolk on top of the trout mix.

6) Finish the plate with a ring of Horseradish-Grain Mustard Vinaigrette and a tuft of micro greens or small herb salad to conceal the egg yolk partially.

Bardog Tavern has taken the lead in Memphis in offering high quality dining in a bar/tavern setting. The Commercial Appeal describes Bardog as "a cut above." I agree. You'll find some predictable items, like the Meatball Hoagie, but this hoagie is outstanding! The bread they use…Wow, they may not make it, but they sure know where to get it. Owner Aldo Dean and his grandmother have put the stamp of their Italian heritage on the fare: Aldo's grandmother actually trained the staff to prepare Bardog's Spaghetti and Meatballs. The Original Memphis Sliders are popular. Check the daily special: I had some scallops so delicious that world class chefs like Jean-George Vongerichten or Daniel Boulud would have asked about them. Offered daily: Ahi Sushi Tuna on Wontons. Private non-smoking banquet room; catering; downtown delivery. By the way, Aldo knows his sliders: On the menu at Aldo's Slider Inn on Peabody Avenue, The Low Rider looks enticing: marinated chicken, caramelized onions, avocado, white American cheese and Sriracha aioli. The Slider Inn is Aldo's latest business venture; the latest addition to the Aldo Dean family is their precious daughter, Luca Mare Dean.

Beer Cheese Soup

Yield: About 10 servings

Ingredients:
4 stalks celery, diced
½ onion, diced
3 cloves garlic, minced
1 pt GUINNESS®
2 qts heavy cream
½ cup cornstarch (you may substitute roux)
1 cup cold chicken stock
1 lb grated cheddar cheese

Directions:

In a large heavy bottomed pot, sweat celery, onion and garlic over low to medium heat for 5-10 minutes. Vegetables should soften a bit, but not brown.

Continuing to cook, stir in GUINNESS®.

Whisk in heavy cream and bring just to a simmer.

In a small bowl, combine cornstarch and cold chicken stock; whisk until smooth, to make a slurry.

Drizzle the slurry into the soup, whisking to incorporate.

Simmer soup gently and briefly: Soup will begin to thicken.

Whisk in grated cheese and bring soup back to a simmer.

Season with salt and pepper and serve.

Tomato Bisque

Yield: About 10 servings

Ingredients:
2 32 oz cans crushed tomatoes
1 32 oz can tomato sauce
2 qts heavy cream
1 Tbs salt

Combine all ingredients in a large pot and simmer gently for about 15 minutes, stirring occasionally. Enjoy!

Belmont Grill

9102 Poplar Pike Germantown, TN

624-6001 www.belmontgrillgermantown.com

The Belmont Grill on Poplar Pike at Forest Hill-Irene in Germantown is a true neighborhood pub, one of the few Germantown restaurants that is an independent, locally owned and managed business. Menu items are prepared in house, even soups and sauces; your food is cooked to order. The extensive menu has a pronounced Southern drawl: Black-eyed Pea Dip, Sausage Po' Boy, Catfish Po' Boy, BBQ Shrimp, a delicious Shrimp Bisque. Regulars often stop by on Sundays for fried chicken and lemon icebox pie. The Grilled Portobello Mushroom Sandwich is a popular item, not just for vegetarians. If you're in the mood for something that's not on the menu, just ask: These friendly folks will try to accommodate. Although the Belmont Grill @ Germantown is no longer affiliated with the Belmont Grill on Poplar in Memphis, the two Belmonts still manage to serve the same savory, award-winning, dog-gone good hamburger, The Belmont Burger: charbroiled choice ground beef with your choice of cheese on a French roll. Both Belmonts are open daily for lunch and dinner, except for Thanksgiving, Christmas, Super Bowl Sunday and the 4th of July.

Portobello Mushroom Sandwich

Yield: 6 sandwiches

6 large portobello mushroom caps
Seasoned Oil (recipe below)
6 slices of tomato
Cheese Mixture (recipe below)
6 slices of Jack cheese
Grated Parmesan for garnish
6 ciabatta rolls

Method:

Drizzle Seasoned Oil over both sides of mushroom caps.

Charbroil mushroom caps, stem side up, for approximately 3 minutes.

Flip caps over and charbroil for 2 additional minutes, stem side down.

Flip caps back to stem side up.

Place 1 slice of tomato in each cap; add a portion of Cheese Mixture and top with 1 slice of Jack cheese.

To Plate:

Garnish filled mushroom cap with a little grated Parmesan. Halve ciabatta roll lengthwise and place filled mushroom cap between the two halves. Slice sandwich diagonally and serve.

Seasoned Oil

Ingredients:
½ cup olive oil blend
¼ cup balsamic vinegar
2 Tbs plus ¾ tsp pesto
Pinch of salt

Pinch of pepper

Cheese Mixture

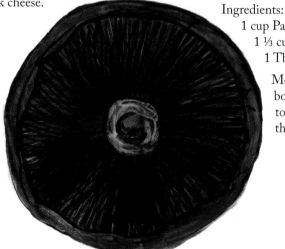

Ingredients:
1 cup Parmesan cheese
1 ⅓ cups ricotta cheese
1 Tbs plus 1 tsp pesto

Method: In a small bowl, stir ingredients together until thoroughly mixed.

2559 Broad Ave. Memphis, TN 730-0719 www.thecovememphis.com

The Cove, with its retro, nautical themed bar specializing in fresh oysters, is a sight to behold. The atmosphere is fun, upbeat, casual and friendly. The Mermaid Salad is The Cove's own version of what some refer to as "The Wedge," and it's scrumptious. The menu offers a variety of pizzas. On Jim's Ultimate Oyster Pizza, definitely a house specialty, you'll get artichokes, goat cheese, bacon, fresh oysters and spinach Rockefeller sauce. Among the panini, there's "The Cove": Genoa, soppressata and coppa salami with Italian olive salad and provolone cheese on ciabatta. The "Plates" are tempting: Argos Gyro, Mediterranean Veggie Platter, The Popeye Pita and my favorite, Stoner Pie. Desserts draw my attention: Chocolate Truffle or Blonde Butter Brownie. Live music regularly, Thursday through Saturday. For who's playing, check the After Dark Live Music Schedule of the Memphis Flyer. (Note: The Cove welcomes patrons "21 and older — meaning yes, smoking is allowed!")

Stoner Pies

Yield: 6 individual casseroles

Stoner Pies are great make-ahead items. Prepared in advance, they can be heated and ready to serve in just minutes.

Basic Ingredients:
12 defrosted LaRosa Tamales* The REAL Tamale™
16 oz cream cheese
2 small cans (10 oz) RO*TEL® Original Diced Tomatoes & Green Chilies
Fresh ground cumin to taste
Olive oil
Garnishes:
6 large scoops of FRITOS® Corn Chips
6 fresh parsley sprigs

Materials and Equipment: 6 individual (8 oz) oval casseroles; a double boiler; plastic wrap or foil.

Prepare in Advance:

Lightly brush individual oval casseroles with olive oil.

In the top of a double boiler over hot water, melt and mix together the cream cheese and RO*TEL®. Remove from heat and set aside.

Cut each defrosted tamale horizontally into two pieces, one piece slightly longer than the other.

Place 2 long pieces of tamale side by side, lengthwise, in each mini casserole. At each end of the 2 long pieces of tamale, place a short piece of tamale, crosswise.

Divide the cream cheese/RO*TEL® mixture evenly among the 6 casseroles.

Press the warm cream cheese mixture into the crevices around the tamales, making sure to cover the tamales completely.

Sprinkle fresh ground cumin over each casserole.

Let the pies cool to room temperature.

Cover with plastic wrap or foil and refrigerate.

Heat and Serve:

Microwave instructions: Unwrap and heat each serving for 2½ minutes.

Conventional oven instructions: Preheat oven to 475 degrees, unwrap casseroles and bake for 8 minutes.

Garnish each heated casserole with a fresh parsley sprig and serve with a large scoop of FRITOS® on the side.

*Made in Memphis, these tamales are available at Charlie's Meat Market at 4790 Summer Avenue, or at www.larosatamales.com.

Earnestine & Hazel's

531 S. Main Memphis, TN 523-9754

Character laden and reportedly haunted, Earnestine & Hazel's is located in a 100-year old building in the lively South Main Historic District. Earnestine & Hazel's takes pride in its legendary (and haunted?) jukebox stocked with the best in blues, jazz and country favorites. Near the jukebox is an appropriately spacious dance floor. Hamburger lovers rave over Earnestine & Hazel's famous Soul Burger. If you are in the mood for a romantic dinner, make your way beyond the bar and the dance floor to The 5 Spot, an intimate, classy restaurant-inside-the-restaurant that seats maybe 12 diners. I can imagine Lauren Bacall and Humphrey Bogart enjoying a quiet dinner here. Oh, by the way, the food is superb!

Grilled Cilantro and Lime Shrimp

Yield: 3 main course servings from 1½ lbs jumbo shrimp
(This recipe can be expanded successfully to serve a crowd.)

Ingredients:
1½ lbs jumbo shrimp*
Olive oil
Diced onions
Freshly chopped cilantro
1 Tbs capers
Fresh cloves of garlic, minced
Minced ginger
Dab of local honey
Some lemon zest
Some lemon juice
Crushed black pepper
Kosher salt
Pinch of cayenne
A little white wine

Note on Seasonings: Except for proportion of capers to shrimp (1 Tbs capers to 1½ lbs jumbo shrimp), simply use listed ingredients to season shrimp according to preference.

Garnishes: Fresh lemon and lime juice; fresh lemon and lime slicesSide Dish: Couscous (recipe below)

Preparation:

Peel and devein shrimp.

In a large cast iron skillet, combine all seasonings with olive oil, add shrimp, place skillet on hot charcoal grill and cover skillet.

Keep an eye on the shrimp and stir them up a bit: Once the skillet heats up, the shrimp will cook VERY quickly. As soon as the shrimp turn pink and opaque, remove them from the heat. Do not overcook!

Transfer shrimp with sauce to serving platter or to individual plates. Sprinkle with a mixture of fresh lemon and lime juice. Garnish with fresh lemon and lime slices and serve with prepared couscous.

Couscous

Ingredients:
Bell peppers, cut into strips
Olive oil
Cooked couscous
Fresh rosemary leaves, minced
Italian parsley, minced
Lemon zest

Preparation:

Sauté bell pepper strips in olive oil, toss with cooked couscous, rosemary. Italian parsley and lemon zest.

*The standard count for jumbo shrimp is 11-15 per pound.

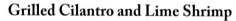

Chef's Recommendations: Best wine pairing–[yellow tail]® Chardonnay, from The Corkscrew, of course; best dessert--one of the awesome varieties of cheesecake made by Kevin Matthews down at The Cheesecake Corner.

89

The Art of Dining in Memphis 2 is the fourth publication in Joy Bateman's series, The Art of Dining*. Longtime Senior Account Executive for Memphis magazine, Joy is a best-selling local author who illustrates and publishes her own work. She is the daughter of Joyce and Lester Gingold, a couple known for their creativity and expertise in the arts and in journalism. Joyce is a visual artist currently making sculpture. Lester has been active in media and retail sales since the 1940's; he currently publishes The Best Times. Joy has passed the creative genes to her three children: Anna Wunderlich, an accomplished painter; Brown Burch, sous-chef at NYC's Picholine, a Michelin-starred restaurant; and William Bateman, performing artist and future lawyer. Joy enjoys cooking and drawing with her young grandsons. She and her husband both enjoy spending time with the youngest set, playing baseball and going to movies, plays and the zoo.

*Previous titles in the series: The Art of Dining in Memphis (2005), The Art of Dining in New Orleans (2007) and The Art of Dining in Nashville (2009).

Cupcakes go way back, farther than you'd think —
I can tell you the story in one quick wink:
In 1796, cakes "baked in small cups"
Appeared in America's first book for cooks--
Writer Amelia Simmons gave instructions for baking.
In 1828, Eliza Leslie did the naming:
She called the sweets "cupcakes" in her own book, *Receipts*.
Move ahead a hundred years: Say "Hello" to Hostess®
treats.
To the plain chocolate icing on the Hostess® original,
Baker "Doc" Rice added little white squiggles. Making
Hostess® stand out was his personal mission:
He got a spot in pop history for his fifties addition.
Hostess® CupCakes were my childhood choice.
Chocolate and creamy and very moist.
Now look all around: You'll be amazed at the craze.
Gourmet cupcakes have taken center stage.
Now in the limelight at restaurant Flight,
The small, dainty cakes are a tasty delight.
Many colors, many flavors, all sweet and mild:
Creative bakers are going wild.
A cake designed to serve just one.
Try two, try three (or more!) for fun.
Cupcakes large, cupcakes small,
Cupcakes short, cupcakes tall.
Every kind of cupcake under the sun:
Dreamsicle, strawberry, lemon, even rum.
Discerning diners consider them posh.
Utensils never needed, no plates to wash.
Cupcakes are popping up everywhere.
(Wish they were as healthful as a pear!)
With that said, let's go to bed…

And dream of cupcakes.

Joy Bateman

www.joysartofdining.com